Little
goes a long way

Little
goes a long way
My own story

Syd Little

HarperCollins*Publishers*

HarperCollins*Publishers*
77–85 Fulham Palace Road, London W6 8JB

First published in Great Britain in 1999 by
HarperCollins*Publishers*

1 3 5 7 9 10 8 6 4 2

A catalogue record for this book
is available from the British Library.

ISBN 000 274014 1

Printed and bound in Great Britain by
Caledonian International Book Manufacturing Ltd, Glasgow

Contents

1

Happy days

'There's a place up north called Blackpool, that's full of fresh air and fun...' That well-known saying comes from a famous ode called 'Albert and the Lion'. It's a poem about a young boy who gets eaten by a lion at Blackpool Zoo. The thing about Blackpool is that you either love it or loathe it, and it's always been the butt of many gags. One of them starts something like this: 'On a Friday night you can walk along the Golden Mile on a carpet of chips.' Or, 'I wouldn't say the sea's dirty, but I remember my mum taking me on the beach as a child and shouting, "Cyril, come out of that water, you've just had a bath!" '

Then, of course, there are the famous Blackpool landladies. I knocked on the door of a bed and breakfast place and the landlady opened the window.

'What do you want?' she asked.

'I want to stay here,' I replied.

'Well, stay there then!' she said, as she closed the window.

When I went down for breakfast in the morning I said, 'Waitress, there's a crack in my plate!'

'That's your bacon!' she answered.

Then I asked her what was on the menu for tea. 'Running Buffy,' she said.

'What's that?' I asked.

'Epsom salts sandwiches!'

Blackpool is also famous for its tower, the lights and the rock, which reminds me of a true story. Back in the 1960s there was an entrepreneur from Liverpool (where else!) and he was talking to his children about their holiday in Spain. He asked them if they'd remembered to buy him some rock, but they told him no one sold it there. In a flash of inspiration the man went to Blackpool and ordered a truckload of rock, with 'Spain' printed through the centre. Thinking he was about to make his fortune, he drove the truck to Dover, travelled on a boat to Calais and then made his way down to the Spanish border. When the border guards inspected the truck they naturally discovered hundreds of little pink sticks. Because they'd never seen rock before, they assumed it was dynamite, so they drove the truck to some wasteland and blew the whole thing up!

To a lot of people, Blackpool is a grotty place, but some people do love it and I'm one of them because I was born there on 19 December 1942. I'm what's known as a 'Sandgrown'n' – that's someone born in Blackpool. (If you were born in Bolton, you'd be a 'Bolton Trotter', and if you were born in Devon you'd be a 'Devon Dumpling'.)

Happy days

The war was on and my mother was sent to Blackpool to have me because bombs were dropping on Manchester, where she lived. It wasn't long before we were back home, though. Mum originally told me that I was born in a place called the Angel Hotel, but it wasn't until I was in my twenties that I discovered this was her idea of a joke!

I was christened Cyril John Mead, but I've also been called Syd, Scissors and Cy, and some other names that I daren't mention in this book. There were six in our family – myself, my parents, my brother Peter, who is two years older than me, and the twins David and Linda, who are six years younger. Our first home was at 2 Hatfield Avenue, Burnage. Burnage is now very famous because it's the birthplace of the Gallagher brothers (as in Oasis).

My Dad, Cyril, was in the RAF during the war and Mum said that I cried when he first came home. Mind you, I was only two years old and Peter couldn't even remember him. Coming home must have been a real shock for my Dad, because one minute he was in the Burmese jungle and the next he's surrounded by his wife and kids. In fact my brother told me that Dad did find it hard to adjust to home life and that's why he drank. I know this was true because he used to come home drunk – well, not exactly drunk, but certainly merry.

I can remember one Sunday lunch-time when my Dad, who'd had a few, started rambling on about bayonets and hand-to-hand fighting. His wartime memories were always recounted when he was drunk. Anyway, he suddenly stood up and told Peter to go to the back door, and then he threw

3

this enormous carving knife at him – which luckily landed between his legs. As you can imagine, my Mum went berserk. In fact I don't think she talked to Dad for ages after that incident and I can't say that I blame her.

Later on in my life that same knife nearly caused a second disaster. Peter and I were using it to make a bow and arrows out of branches and he was choppping off twigs while I held onto the other end. Yes, you've guessed it: he sliced my finger as well and I've got the scars to prove it. Being just a young lad, I went running into Mum screaming my head off. Unfortunately my Mum couldn't stand the sight of blood, so she wrapped a towel around my hand and sent me to our neighbour. It was a good thing that our neighbour wasn't so squeamish, and she attended to my wound.

When my Dad returned to Civvy Street he worked as an electrician for an American firm called Carburundum. The most memorable feature of this firm for me was their Christmas parties. I'll always remember Dad dressing up as Father Christmas and handing out presents to the children. I'm sure there was a bit of favouritism going on, because I always got the best one!

A few years later, when he switched jobs to work as a steeplejack, he was commissioned to dress up as Father Christmas again – but this time he had to land on top of the Lewis store, which was built like a skyscraper. After landing he had to climb down a golden ladder while hundreds of people watched and cheered him. And all the time I was thinking to myself, 'That's my Dad up there.' I felt so proud of him and I wanted to shout his real identity at the top of my voice, but Mum put paid to that. She said, 'The children think that your Dad is the real Father Christmas so don't spoil things for them.'

Now don't cry for me, but I remember in my early years that I never got a birthday present. This was because I was born so close to Christmas. Mum's excuse was that I'd get something bigger and better for Christmas instead, and every year I fell for the same line.

It's a funny thing, but somehow I can always remember my Christmas holidays quite clearly, whereas my summer memories seem to be more vague. However, there was one great summer that I'll never forget. Mum was expecting the twins so Peter and I were sent to Uncle Arthur, who lived just outside Stockport. Uncle Arthur and Auntie Esther weren't our blood relatives; they were just good friends with Mum and Dad. We stayed with them because they owned a farm. Uncle Arthur was a proper countryman with a rugged red face. He had two children of his own and two foster boys, but I can't remember any of their names. The farm was more of a small-holding, really, with a variety of animals – chickens, cows, pigs and a huge horse called Dolly. I can remember the wonderful experience of climbing onto her back and being led round the farm with four other youngsters.

During my stay at the farm that year, Uncle Arthur had to take his sow to the abattoir and I'm convinced she knew where she was going. I can still see my Dad and my two uncles, George (who I'll tell you about later) and Arthur, trying to catch the animal. They were trying to put her into the truck, but the pig kicked and butted and then ran between my Dad's legs, knocking him over. The loudest sound came from my Uncle George, who was killing himself with laughter. Watching their antics made me realize that I didn't want the happy summer to end.

After the holidays I had to start at Greenends, my primary school. My first memory is of playing in a big tin bath. We had to learn what pints, quarts and gallons were and I was obviously well taught because I can still remember them all to this day. In the afternoons we were given a Farleys rusk and orange juice and then told to have a sleep on little camp-beds. We were meant to stay there for a whole hour. Well, could I sleep? Of course not! But when the teacher came round and saw me still awake I suddenly felt very tired...

Because I was good at art I enjoyed going to school. In fact, one of my paintings which showed St George and the Dragon was hung in the headmaster's study. I was actually very upset about this because I wanted it for my Mum and Dad! One of the teachers at Greenends was called Miss Lucas. I think she liked me because one day she asked if she could see the twins, who'd just been born. When she arrived at our house she gave my Mum a bottle of calamine lotion, and to this day I'm not quite sure what it was for.

Looking back, it was a real bonus to have an older brother to protect me. I can remember going to the pictures one Saturday morning (it cost just ninepence to see Flash Gordon. I thought he was brilliant!). We used to cut across the grammar school grounds and go behind my school to reach the picture house. On this particular morning there was a gang of lads hiding behind the dustbins and they came rushing out to fight us. Peter bashed a couple of them while I cowered behind him and they soon scattered.

Although Peter was small he was a tough little critter, but I have to confess that I wasn't always very nice to him when we were growing up. We were having dinner on one occasion and I pinched some chips off his plate, so naturally he snatched them back. Unfortunately for Peter my Dad saw him, smacked him and sent him to bed. I never said a word. Mind you, I think I made up for it later.

When I was eight we moved to Wythenshawe. It must have been September time, because I befriended a lad called John Richardson and we went to the local park on our bikes collecting conkers. During my childhood Wythenshawe Park was one of my favourite haunts. I remember going into the woods there on my own to play Robin Hood and I used to make a den out of fern leaves. Ferns always remind me of my childhood. The park was quite safe then, and it's sad to think that children can't play on their own today like I did then. I was brought up in the days when people used to say, 'You can leave your back door open and you won't get burgled around here.' What we have to remember, I suppose, is that people had nothing to pinch in those days! Now we all own videos, TVs and CD players.

Although my Dad was a qualified electrician, he was a bit of a jack-of-all-trades. And because he was good at so many things he was able to change jobs frequently. This meant he turned his hand to bricklaying, electrical work, hod-carrying and even a stint as a steeplejack, as I mentioned before. Dad was also quite musical and he was good at playing the squeeze-box – or accordion, for those of you unfamiliar with this term. I think it was his influence that gave me a love for music – but more of that later.

As far as my Mum's work was concerned, she started as a cleaner in a church across the road from us called St Michael's All Angels. She stayed there for about four years and I can remember her telling me that she used to talk to God while she scrubbed the floors. What she talked to Him about I'll never know. One day she was cleaning under a big cross that used to hang from the church ceiling. Looking up at it, she noticed that it was suspended on a very thin piece of rope, and she suddenly said to herself, 'Oh, my God!' What she didn't know was that the vicar was standing right behind her, and he replied, 'Oh, Mrs Mead!' Well, that incident must have frightened her off because she never went under that cross again.

After the church my Mum was employed as a Hoffman presser. As far as I can remember, the presser looked like two giant ironing boards, one on top of the other. The two boards were brought together and pressed whatever was inside them with a big gust of steam. I remember watching Mum work the thing one day and I couldn't believe that she could use such a massive machine – she was only four foot eleven! I think she must have been standing on a box to work it. Anyway, she stuck it out until she was 65 because the owners kept calling her back as she did the job so well. I can recall that she was on piecework, which meant that you got paid for how much you did, rather than the number of hours you worked.

During this period of my life I'd started my first job as a paper boy. I was offered the grand total of 6s. 6d. per week. Along with my earnings I got two comics, *The Lion* and *The Tiger*, a Mars bar and a box of Smarties. The newsagent that I worked for was quite strict and insisted that we worked every night and Sunday mornings. And you had to be there for six o'clock if you wanted your wages. After my Sunday paper round I went home to cook breakfast for all the family. I really enjoyed doing this because I was always starving by then. I'd fry eggs, bacon, tomatoes – the lot – but no one got up very early on Sunday mornings so I think I usually ate most of it myself.

One of the saddest moments in my young life involved a collie dog that had followed Peter home from the park. She was a well-behaved animal and had obviously come from a good home. After the dog had been in our house for two days Mum told us that we had to report her to the police in case some little old lady was crying her eyes out over the loss.

Because I was doing my paper round, Mum said, 'You pass the police station, Cyril, so you pop in and tell them about Queenie (that's what we'd nicknamed the dog).'

Queenie followed me on my paper round and when I got to the police station she walked through the door behind me. Looking up at this massive policeman at the desk, I said, 'I've come to report a missing dog.'

'Do you want us to take the dog in?' he asked.

Being nervous, I just said 'Yes' rather quickly.

When I got home Peter, David and Linda were having their tea. 'Where's Queenie?' they chorused.

'The policeman took her off me,' I replied.

'Why didn't you ask if you could keep her until she was claimed?' Mum asked.

When I told them that I'd been nervous and hadn't stopped to think about keeping her, a big argument broke out. In the end they told me that I had to go and get her. But I said I was hungry and that she'd still be there tomorrow.

The following day I saw the same policeman at the station. 'Can I take Queenie home now?' I asked. It was then that he said she'd been taken to the pound, but that I wasn't to worry because they kept dogs there for weeks before they put them down. He suggested that I called in there the following day. When I arrived home Mum said that I might as well leave the dog until the weekend.

Saturday came and we went to the pound and asked for Queenie. The reply completely devastated me. The policeman said she'd been put down. Growing desperate, I said, 'You can't have done that because you said you kept dogs for at least a fortnight!'

'Well,' he said, 'it depends when the vet calls. Unfortunately he came early.'

I wanted to believe that there had been some awful mistake, but I knew in my heart that Queenie was dead. In the eyes of Peter, David and Linda I was guilty of murder and, what was worse, I kept blaming myself. If only I'd asked on that first visit if I could have kept her this might never have happened. The memory of that whole incident still hurts today.

However, you might say that we were never very good with pets. I remember we had three cats, at different times. The first never came home, but just disappeared, another got run over and the third had an abscess on its face. Peter and I decided we ought to take this third cat to the vet to see if there was anything he could do. Wrapping the cat in a blanket, we boarded a number 50 bus and when the conductor came along he asked if he could see our cat. We pulled the blanket back a bit.

'Well,' said the conductor, 'if I were you, lads, I'd get off at the next stop and go home.'

When we asked him what he meant he replied, 'Because your cat's dead!'

Immediately, we both burst out crying. Mind you, we *had* noticed that the cat was a bit stiff! So I have to say that my experiences with animals have taught me that it's best not to have them as pets, because in the end it's a heartache you can do without.

Apart from my dealings with pets I had a happy childhood and I enjoyed the company of some great mates. Ronnie Barlow was one of them. His Dad used to build push-bikes and I think everyone in the area had one. They were popular because none of us could afford the new ones in the shops. Mr Barlow used to get the frames from the rubbish tip, or wherever he could find them, and respray the parts. By the time he'd added the wheels the bikes were as good as new.

Another childhood friend of mine was a smart lad called John Storey. I'll always remember him because one day we were out playing with my Dinky toys, skidding them along the pavement and getting them all scratched and dented, when John said, 'I've got Dinky toys, but my Mum won't let me play with them.'

Being a kid, I naturally thought he was making this up until he asked his Mum if he could show me his collection. Well, he had been telling the truth because there they were, all boxed up and in immaculate condition. I bet he's still got them today and they're probably worth a fortune. My father-in-law is always saying to my young son Dominic, 'Always keep toys that are made of metal or wood because they could become collector's items.' So now our loft is full of boxes!

Strangely enough, I seemed to get on better with girls at this time of my life than when I was older. As a teenager and in my early twenties I was useless. I think being a seven-stone weakling with National Health glasses (you know those little wire ones) didn't help my appearance. I could never afford the fashionable clothes of the day – like a teddy-boy outfit – and my failed crew cut didn't exactly boost my morale. I tried really hard to get my hair to stand up by using Brylcream and Vaseline, but nothing worked. I ended up looking like a monkey!

Anyway, back to my younger days for the moment, and two friends called Christine and Lillian Kemp. They lived in Kern Grove, just across the road from my house. I remember that their Mum had an illness – I think it was leukaemia – and she had a bed downstairs. When the weather wasn't good enough for us to play outside we'd sit with her and

listen to the radio (we didn't have a television). One programme which has stuck in my mind was a play called *The
Kraken Wakes*. It was about a sea monster that attacked ships
and then wrecked them. I've since discovered that this is a bit
of Greek mythology, but at the time I was scared to death.

Our neighbours in Moorcroft Road were the Butter-
worths – Ted and Doris, I think they were called. They had
a daughter called Norma and she was like a big sister to me.
I never looked on her as 'just another girl' because she was
quite ladylike. She had a bubbly personality, a shock of red
hair and a freckled face.

Mum and Dad smoked and I remember that they used to
leave just a tab at the end of the cigarettes and store these in
a cocoa tin. When the tin was full Peter would take it round
to Ted Butterworth, who smoked a pipe. He would remove
the paper seal from the tab-ends and use the tobacco, which
meant he could smoke for nothing. Peter and Norma would
meet in the alleyway between our two houses and they
would smoke too. They'd pinch the biggest ends for themselves and leave the rest for Ted. I don't think their respec-
tive parents know to this day what they were up to then!

Another incident with Norma happened just after bonfire
night one year. There had been a big display in
Wythenshawe Park and the following morning Peter and I
were looking for rocket sticks. During our search we found
one at the same time and started arguing over it.

Suddenly Norma appeared and said, 'What's going on?'

'It's my stick!' I said.

'No, it's not, it's mine!' Peter answered back.

Norma immediately took control of the situation, got hold of the stick and broke it in half. 'There, half each, end of story,' she said.

Some years later Norma married a handsome young man, a fitness fanatic called Harold Bates. I can recall seeing him in her backyard with his weights. One day when he was training he got me to lift them. Somewhere there's a photo of me doing just that and you can see my entire rib cage! I have to say that I'm still a seven-stone weakling and hopeless with weights.

As well as keeping fit, Harold was great at jiving, as were Norma, my brother Peter and his girlfriend Sonia (now his wife). Norma and Harold would jive in our front room to 'Let's have a party' by Elvis Presley, but it was Peter and Sonia who won an 11-hour jive marathon at the Sale Locarno. I don't think he could jive for 11 *minutes* today!

I was more interested in music than jiving and up until this point in my life my tastes had been *Uncle Mac* on the radio and *Children's Choice*, with tunes like 'The runaway train', 'Sparky's magic piano' and 'The king's new clothes' by Danny Kaye. But then along came rock'n'roll – wow! It seemed as if Elvis, Little Richard and Bill Haley had been invented for us teenagers. The grown-ups hated it and naturally that made it even better. Even the Church said it was the devil's music, but later on Cliff Richard released a song that asked, 'Why should the devil have all the good music?'

Influenced by this new sound, I saw an advert in the *Daily Mirror* that read: 'Buy Your Welcome To Britain Elvis Guitar, 7s. 6d.' Well, that was for me. I sent my money off straight away and for the next fortnight I'd rush home from school and ask Mum if it had arrived. She must have got fed up saying 'No', because when she did I'd get really upset.

Eventually one morning it did arrive, but when I opened the package I was terribly disappointed. The guitar was so small and with just four strings it was more like a ukulele. It had a picture of Elvis Presley on the front and 'Welcome to Britain' printed underneath. Seeing my glum face, Mum said, 'What did you expect for 7s. 6d?'

I was determined that I hadn't wasted my money, however, so I asked Dad to tune the guitar. Singing a little song he later taught me, called 'My dog has fleas', he tuned the instrument to his vocal pitch. I quickly learnt three basic chords, G, C and D, but my family soon got fed up with my strumming and I was running out of places to play. Eventually I found the perfect solution – our loo. It had two doors, so it was quite soundproof and it also gave a good echo effect. I spent many hours sitting there and the song that I practised over and over again was 'Nothing to do and nowhere to go, no one to listen to my tale of woe' by Michael Holiday. From those humble beginings I was hooked. After Michael Holiday I started listening to Lonny Donegan and I found I could play his songs very easily, because all you needed to know was three basic chords.

Before long I wanted to start a skiffle group. I can't remember who it was, but one of my mates – Alf or Fred Claire or Tony Kemple (there were too many to mention them all) – had a washboard and I had the guitar (well, the ukulele), so all we needed was a tea-chest bass.

For you younger readers, a tea-chest bass consists of a big plywood box (like a packing case) with an open end. The boxes were originally used to transport tea from India. You also needed a broom handle and a long piece of string or wire. You placed the chest on the ground, open side down, and made a small hole in the top to secure the wire in place. The broom handle was placed in one corner on the top of the box and the wire taken up and tied to the top of the handle. As the handle was moved about and the wire plucked you were able to produce a bass note. It may sound primitive, but this instrument was taken very seriously by the players. They were very fussy about the type of chest they used and its country of origin. Then there was the size of the hole that you made and the strength of the wire. It was a real science getting the sound right.

Well, we didn't have a tea chest but Alf and Fred's grandma did, so I said, 'Great, let's go and get it!' We lived in Wythenshawe and their gran lived near the Strangeways prison in north Manchester, about eight miles away. The only transport we had was our bikes, so we planned a cycle ride to retrieve this box. What we forgot to calculate was the size of the tea chest. It was bigger than most of us and we didn't stop to consider how awkward it might be to move. In the end Tony Kemple took his tandem – he and Fred rode that, followed by a convoy of 10 bikes. When we arrived Tony tied the tea chest on his back and started off home, swapping with Fred about four miles into the journey. It must have looked very funny when we finally got back home, because there were 10 kids just standing looking at this tea chest. We had a few sessions with it in the back garden (they weren't too bad, I suppose), but then it got wet because Mum wouldn't let me bring it inside, so that was the end of the skiffle group.

One Christmas – it must have been when I was about 14 years old – I went round knocking on doors for my paper round Christmas box. I collected £4.10s. When I got home I gave it to Mum and told her to put it aside for my new guitar and, bless her cotton socks, she said she would make up the balance. Well, I felt 10 feet tall because my dream of owning a proper instrument was about to come true.

The following Saturday Alf, Tony and myself took the train to Altrincham and I went into the music shop there called White and Swales. (For any Manchester City fans, the Swales was none other than Peter Swales, who used to be the chairman of the club for a while.) Looking back, I wish I'd had some advice before buying that first guitar. A while ago, when Eddie and I were doing our television show, I was chatting with Hank Marvin (one of my all-time heroes) and he said, 'Never buy the first one you try.' Mind you, I only had eight guineas with me that day in Swales, which didn't give me a great deal of choice anyway.

I ended up with a Spanish guitar and it did have six strings! Those extra two baffled me for a while and to start with I just played the top four like a ukulele. I also found that after a couple of days my fingers were really sore and I ended up with grooves on them, because metal strings don't give like nylon ones. John Lennon shouts on one of his records, 'I've got blisters on my fingers!' – well, I knew what he meant! Whenever I hear that record it always reminds me of those days. Still, after a few weeks of practice I got a nice little repertoire together, all three-chord stuff and mostly skiffle tunes like 'Cumberland gap', and 'Does your chewing gum lose its flavour on the bed-post overnight?' – what a title!

At Christmas my Dad always took his accordion to the Sale Hotel, which was his local boozer, and this particular year was no exception. During the Christmas period the landlords used to turn a blind eye if there were a few young teenagers about, especially if they were with their parents. So yours truly took his trusty guitar and his mate Fred Claire to the hotel. It was a big pub with a concert room, a snug, a few side rooms and a vault. The vault was where all the men gathered – women were definitely not allowed in! (Mind you, I think they are today.) This was where my Dad always went, so I just followed him.

After a few pints had gone down (I didn't participate because I was too young – honest) Dad got on his squeeze-box and started to play, and he was good. He was into The Ink Spots, Glenn Miller and '40s songs, anything from the war years, in fact. There were quite a few young men and teenagers in the vault on this particular night, though, and they didn't care for my Dad's sort of music. So I was asked to play something a bit more modern – 'Singing the blues' and that sort of thing, which I could manage with three chords! They didn't have to ask me twice and the evening developed into a 'them' and 'us' contest. I remember our

Peter being wheelbarrowed by this big fellow, Bob Brooks, and chalking a line down the centre of the room. The line split us in half, with my Dad and his mates on one side and me and all the younger people on the other.

We took it in turns to perform, Dad and I. Looking back now, I did surprisingly well using only three chords. In the end word got round that there was music in the vault and the place was packed out. Peter and Fred collected money in pint pots and when we arrived home later that night we shared out our ill-gotten gains.

I think it was that night, more than any other, that gave me my first taste for show business. It wasn't the money: it was the buzz I felt when I played in front of an audience. There's a show-biz saying, 'If you want to do it don't, but if you've got to do it then persevere.' That was me.

As a young teenager I was a member of the Rackhouse Youth Club and I used to go there two or three times a week. Happy days! I was really able to enjoy myself because I used their tape recorder (one of the old reel-to-reel types) and I'd accompany myself on guitar. I hated the sound of my own voice even then, and I still do, but it didn't put me off. Fortunately my mates Tony, Fred and Johnny seemed to think my vocalizing was okay, so they gave me the confidence to keep going.

One night there was a talent competition and because I was the only member with a guitar I ended up backing most of the performers. In the end I actually won with a rendition of 'Peggy Sue', and the second prize went to a lad called George McDevitte singing the Lonny Donegan number

'The Wabash cannonball'. George split his second-place win-nings with me, so I made an extra two shillings out of him. The three girls who came third singing 'Seven little girls sit-ting in the back seat with Fred' also gave me sixpence, so I collected a total of 7s. 6d. for one night's work, which I thought wasn't bad.

Although the money was useful it was the music that I really enjoyed. By now I knew four chords and being able to play the guitar was a real confidence booster. I was hopeless at all the normal things you might do at a youth club, like table tennis, football, or even chatting up the girls! I think I must have been Britain's first karaoke machine, because wherever I went I ended up backing singers, even if the melody had to survive on a three- or four-chord accompaniment!

2

Let the good times roll

I left Yew Tree Secondary School in Wythenshawe when I was just 15 years old. While I wasn't the brightest of pupils, I wasn't that dim either because I was placed in a middle stream. However, I left without any qualifications which meant I couldn't apply to be a commercial artist or a chef, two careers I had considered training for. My only option was to go straight to the Youth Employment Office. The first job I was offered was as a plastic mac welder. I lasted the grand total of two weeks. The smell was so pungent that I can even recall it today. Next I went to Burton's the tailors and spent my day brushing dust off the suits. This time I lasted about three weeks. In desperation I ended up as a packer in a mail-order firm.

The position as packer involved a certain amount of paperwork and I remember one man insisting I use my right hand – being left-handed, I didn't find this too easy! My work might have been a lot neater, but it took me twice as long to do it. I've often wondered if I'd have been a better guitarist if I'd learnt to play with my right hand. Anyway, after three months I decided that this job was going nowhere so I went back to the employment office.

By now I'd come to the decision that I should get a trade behind me. I thought perhaps I would like to be a plumber, but there were no vacancies. There was an opening with a painter and decorator, however. I reasoned that I was good at art so perhaps I should give it a try. It was a small firm called George Jones & Son, with a father, son and another man called George Johnson. We called him Johnny because there were too many Georges. George Jones Senior was a jolly chap, and he created an easy-going atmosphere. Our work took us into every type of home, from the upper-class houses in Didsbury or Sale in Manchester right down to the new housing estates, which were still empty at that time.

Johnny and I both loved to sing and we looked forward to working in the housing estates because they were unoccupied, and with no one to stop us we could sing to our hearts' content. The empty rooms created wonderful echo chambers.

I can remember one time when I was singing and painting to a slow song, 'Only you' by The Platters, and suddenly George Senior said, 'Syd, will you sing a faster number?'

'Why?' I asked.

'Because your strokes will be faster,' replied George – and do you know what? He was right!

I really enjoyed the years that I spent as a decorator and I stayed in that line of business until I turned professional at

21. By that stage I had almost completed my apprenticeship, with just one year left.

Aside from my work, my social life was quite exciting because I was still so involved in my music, unlike my mates Alf and Tony who only seemed interested in courting. It was about this time that I used to go to the Locarno in Sale. On a Monday night they played all the latest records and this gave me a real taste for rock'n'roll. The Locarno dance floor was divided into sections and on one side you'd have the Wythenshawe gang and on the other you'd have the Moss Side, Sale and Benchill gangs. Naturally everyone stayed in their own group and it was understood that you just didn't mix, but somehow this added to the fun. Being teenagers, there was often a fight and one gang member would pick on a different gang member and it would end up with a full-scale battle. Inevitably we'd get banned, but we'd be back the next week. They were good times.

The Wythenshawe mob consisted of quite a lot of people and our Peter was one of them. Vic Burgess, Bob McDonald and Eddie McGinniss (who became Eddie Large) were also part of the team. Although Eddie lived in Moss Side – or, as he says, 'Greenhase' – he was with the Wythenshawe mob because he played football for the Norbreck Boys' Club in Wythenshawe and he befriended a lot of the local lads. I'll always remember him as he was then because he stood out from the crowd. He had a fantastic teddy-boy outfit with a velvet-collared jacket, drainpipe trousers and, to complete the look, the essential sideburns. No self-respecting teddy boy would be seen without the Elvis Presley sideburns. I was so jealous of Eddie because I could never grow them. I couldn't even achieve a proper crew cut.

If you ask Eddie what impression he had of me in those days you'd be amazed at his reply. He apparently told his mates that I must be really hard because I wore National Health glasses and this horrible baggy suit. Little did he know! Anyway, his opinion didn't prevent us getting together. Eventually his mates Jimmy Brown, Jack Goodwin, Freddy Edwards, Johnny Tie and a few others became friends with my mates and we formed one big gang.

My main ambition at this stage in my life was to own an electric guitar so I was saving like mad. I eventually bought a Hoffner Colourama. Unlike the old ukulele or the Spanish guitar, it gave me real credibility. The Hoffner was a solid guitar and with my portable 10-watt amp I was all set up. Hank Marvin watch out!

One of the first dates that I took my electric guitar to was at the club my Mum and Dad belonged to, called the Brooklands Trade and Labour Club. Because they were members I was allowed in even though I was under age. One night I just got up on stage and accompanied myself on guitar. It must have gone down well because after my first performance they kept inviting me back. I have to say it was a good apprenticeship for me. Although no money changed hands I was grateful for the experience. I used to sing songs like 'My old man's a dustman'.

One night I was performing at the Brooklands and I looked round to see my Dad coming out of the toilets. He was wearing his coat inside out and he'd brushed his hair so that it stuck up all over the place and he'd removed his dentures. This was acceptable behaviour at the club – everyone knew my Dad and they cheered and laughed at his act. About a year later, though, I had accepted a booking at the Timperley Trade and Labour Club (for £3 – wow!) and my Dad came with me. As I walked on stage and started to sing 'My old man's a dustman', my Dad did his usual disappearing act and went into the gents. He emerged a few minutes later, dressed to accompany my performance. Unfortunately, when he stepped up beside me I caught the expression of some of the audience and they were obviously thinking to themselves, 'Who the hell is this nutter?' That reception really affected him and he didn't do the act again. Thinking back, the whole experience was really quite sad, but it taught me that you should never take an audience for granted, especially when you're a newcomer.

As I gained experience in the clubs I realized that my humorous songs were very popular. Songs like 'What a picture', 'My old man's a dustman' and 'Little white bull' were more appreciated than the serious ones, so I decided I should develop my act round humour rather than using ballads.

It was round about this time that Tony Kemple, my old mate from the skiffle group, was going to a pub in Timperley called the Stonemasons Arms every Saturday. If he can get in so can I, I thought, and I knew they staged a 'Free and Easy' night each Saturday with a resident pianist and drummer. So my friend Fred (my first roadie) picked up my amp and off we went. When we arrived we introduced ourselves to the landlady, Mrs Allcock. She must have guessed we were under age (we were about 16 at the time), but she didn't make a fuss and in those days it wasn't considered a very serious offence. Besides, there was nowhere for young people to meet unless they found a youth club, so it was all down to the pubs and clubs.

I told Mrs Allcock that I could play the guitar and she decided to try me out. I plugged in my amp and started to sing and it all went down very well. In fact, I did so well that she said, 'Will you come back next week, and I'll give you a pound?' That's great, I thought to myself, that's me well suited. So nearly every Saturday I performed at the Stonemasons Arms and really enjoyed myself. But the highlight of the evening was closing time. Mrs Allcock used to come round shouting for everybody to drink up and she'd be waving a 12-bore shotgun at the same time. I never discovered whether it was loaded or not, and I'm sure she wouldn't get away with that sort of behaviour today.

All the Wythenshawe mob, including Eddie, discovered that I was working a Saturday night spot, and because it was billed as a 'Free and Easy' night they decided to drop in. Word got round and in no time the pub was filling up with teenagers and most of them were my mates. I'd get up at eight o'clock and sing for about an hour, covering songs by the Drifters and similar artists. When the audience had sunk enough beer, and their confidence had grown (it's called 'Dutch courage'), they would want to get up on stage. So I performed my karaoke act and backed all the other singers, but I have to say that I had a great time. Alf, Tony and

Johnny Haythornwaite would get up to sing and they called themselves the Earwigs. Pretending to be a vocal backing group, they covered numbers by the Everley Brothers. Another mate, Jimmy Bull, always wanted to sing Conway Twitty songs, and finally Eddie would start on a Cliff Richard number – and once he started you couldn't get him off. I think that was the first time he butted in and he's been butting in ever since!

As the audience grew at the Stonemasons things started to get a bit hairy, because we were swamped with so many teenagers that trouble started to break out. One evening after closing time someone smashed a nearby shop window and when the police arrived they told us to go back over the border (Timperley was in Cheshire and Sale was in Manchester) and not to bother coming back.

Mrs Allcock came to my house that weekend and said, 'Sorry Syd, you'll have to find somewhere else, because the police are keeping an eye on my place.' So that was the end of my first real paid performance.

My next venue was at the Royal Oak near Wythenshawe Park, a pub similar to the Stonemasons Arms. My engagement there lasted about six months and I teamed up with Eddie and a mate called Nicky Morris who also played guitar. We'd become friends when he taught me some licks on my guitar. We practised together and learnt some numbers by the Shadows, and we performed these at the Oak. After a few drinks Eddie would join us and before long we were doing a repeat performance of the Stonemasons. The only difference was that this time I didn't get paid. I think all we received after working there every Saturday night for six months was three bottles of brown ale between us.

With all this going on, I had quite a full life as a teenager, and enjoyed the company of my friends. For a hobby we used to go pot-holing most weekends near the Derbyshire border and we'd always end up in a pub. Obsessed with my guitar, I always took it with me on these trips and I'd drag it through some unbelievable places. Our destination was always the vault at a pub called The Lord Nelson and in our soaking wet jeans and anoraks we'd enjoy ourselves with a few drinks.

Between the ages of 16 and 18 I saved up to go to the Isle of Man for a holiday each summer, for the last week in July and the first week in August. In order to prevent myself spending money I used to spend time playing football with my mates in Wythenshawe Park instead, and at the end of July a gang of about 13 lads would take this holiday together.

You can imagine what interests a gang of teenage boys, and we were no different: it was just girls and beer. When we got on the boat the first thing we did was to head straight for the bar. Unfortunately for us, the ship's rules stated that the bar couldn't be opened until the ferry was three miles out to sea, but the moment it was opened everybody started to drink. On a few occasions the crossing was quite rough and I would end up leaning over the side of the boat being sick. I used to have my guitar with me, of course, and I'd sing until I felt too ill to continue and then go up on deck.

We would arrive at Douglas at about six o'clock in the morning and head for our lodgings. We always stayed in a guest house owned by a lady called Mrs Jackson. The whole gang of us would sit on her steps until about ten or eleven o'clock, when our rooms would be ready. We never minded the wait because it was part of the adventure.

The aim of our holiday was simply to have a good time for the entire fortnight. Every Wednesday we went to a talent contest for teenagers at the Villa Marina and Ivy Benson's All-Girl Band would be the backing group. One year, unbeknown to Eddie and myself, our friends had entered us for one of the talent competitions. It was raining that day and so the place was packed; there were even people sitting on the dance floor.

Eventually our names were called out and we had to stand up. As soon as we got to our feet everyone started laughing. I suppose we looked comical because Eddie had put on a little bit of weight and I was as thin as a rake. We made our way to the stage anyway. Ivy Benson was doing a rock'n'roll number and I asked if I could borrow her guitar because on this rare occasion I'd left mine at home.

So there I was, holding this big electric guitar, and Ivy said, 'What are you going to do?'

'Mule skinner blues,' I replied, and Eddie chipped in with, 'Great, we'll do that.'

This was one of my all-time hits and I should have been very confident, but I was so nervous that I started strumming. But 'Mule skinner' is a song that doesn't need any strumming so Eddie had to stop me in midstream and I had

29

to start again. The place was in uproar because they thought this was part of the act and it obviously seemed very funny. Eventually we did the song and we brought the house down, but we had to wait to see what the judges thought.

We were up against a 14-year-old girl with the face of an angel, who'd sung the 'Nuns' Chorus'. She was brilliant and had obviously been professionally trained, and when she finished singing everyone gave her a round of applause. But when our names were mentioned the place erupted and our mates and all the other kids were stamping and banging the floor. The officials kept saying, 'Don't do that. Just applaud, just applaud.' To be honest, I think we should have won the competition, but the girl was so professional that she took the prize. But that day proved to be the start of Eddie and I working together.

Back at home I was offered another gig at the Timperley Trade and Labour Club for £3. My Mum and Dad came with me and so did Eddie. We sat in the audience and watched a group (I can't remember their name) performing. They were trying to copy the Shadows with their fashionable mohair suits and I felt so insignificant wearing the only suit I owned. The group also had fantastic Vox amps, which were 'the' amps of the day, and Fender Stratocastor guitars which I'd have died for.

Finally it was my turn to go on stage and when I did my first spot my amp packed up. Somehow I managed to get through my song and when I came off my Dad, being an electrician, tried to fix the problem. In the meantime I thought to myself, 'I wonder if the lads would lend me one of their amps.' So I went into their room and asked them if they could help me out. None of them would, so I had to take a chance with mine. While I'd been away Dad had been able to do something and my amp was ready for me to use again.

As I was about to do my second spot Eddie said, 'Can I get up with you?' so I said 'Yes'. I was shaking in my shoes, just wondering if the amp was going to pack up again.

Having rehearsed a few numbers together at the Stonemasons and other places, we had a fair idea what we were going to do. We decided to start with a song called 'Rubber ball' and while I sang Eddie would bounce around the stage (there's one thing about Eddie – he can't stand still, he has to be doing something all the time). The place was in uproar over this, so we followed on with 'Mule skinner blues' and finished off with a couple more songs.

That night our act just seemed to gel, and when we came off stage the concert secretary said, 'Right, I'll have you back as a double act and I'll give you £6.' Well, £6 was more than Eddie or I earned for a six-day working week – though we had to split this amount between the two of us, so the £3 I made was the same as I'd been paid for a single act.

After that night things seemed to snowball and we were offered work at various venues around Manchester. The more bookings we took the stronger the act became until finally we were offered a night at the Yew Tree Hotel, which at that time was a prominent venue for Manchester. In fact, I think it was known all over the country. A famous group called the Carl Denver Trio were playing there nearly every week and all the major artists performing in Manchester went to the Yew Tree.

There were some unusual acts around the clubs and pubs in Manchester in those days. You didn't just have singers and comics, which seems to be the norm today; you also had what were called speciality acts. One was called Tommy Toes Jacobsen. Tommy was born without arms and he used to get up on stage and shoot a rifle with his feet and toes and pop a balloon. He would then get a man out of the audience, put a towel round his neck and shave him with a proper cut-throat razor – it was a really good act and you don't see performers like that any more.

Then there was Joe Ruggels, who must have been 70 if he was a day. He was a sort of Tommy Cooper and like Tommy he'd do tricks and they'd go wrong. With Tommy you knew it was supposed to happen, but when Joe did tricks he didn't expect them to go wrong and that's what made it funny.

I remember a comic called Eddie Grant, who's dead now. He was a lovable rogue. He use to perform in the Yew Tree nearly every other week, and he was always cadging money off the landlord, Frank Tansy, and anyone else he could. He'd come with watches and other goods, and try to sell them off; I think Eddie took a pair of cuff links off him, but he never paid for them and I don't think Eddie (Grant) ever realized.

One day he arrived having not turned up for work the week before, and Frank said, 'Where were you last week? You had the money up front and you didn't turn up.'

'It was my mother, Frank, she died,' replied Eddie, and he started to cry and really go over the top.

Frank said, 'Oh, I am sorry to hear that, Eddie, I'm very sorry,' and Eddie Grant got away with it.

He must have had a very short memory because about six weeks later he did the same thing again and tried the same routine and Frank said, '*?!*! Well you owe me. Have you got two mothers or something? You said one died six weeks ago!'

These were just some of the people Eddie and I met as we took our act round the clubs in Manchester, including the Princess and the Domino. We were doing pretty well, and the owner of one of the clubs told us we should ask for more money. He said we were pulling in the audiences and putting the big stars to shame. So we went to Bobby, who was the compere at a club called the Princess, and asked him if we could have a rise. All he did was give us some hard-luck story about how he couldn't afford to, so we accepted his argument and continued to work for the same fee.

While we were working at the Princess and the Domino we discovered that all the well-known pop stars appeared there too. In fact, when we turned semi-profesional we still performed in these clubs and on one occasion we saw the Springfields (Dusty Springfield and her brother). Eddie and I would come on and the place would be in uproar: we'd get a bigger response than the main act and we were still earning a pittance in comparison to everyone else. It didn't really bother us that much, though, because we were just enjoying ourselves.

I remember on one occasion we had just gone down a storm at the Princess and we had to get to the Domino, which was north of Manchester, and we didn't have a car. At the bus stop we were sitting on our amplifiers waiting for the bus and all the people who had just been screaming for us were now standing in the same queue. 'Where's your Rolls-Royce?' they asked, and Eddie had to say, 'Well, it's being repaired.' Little did they know!

Eventually Eddie bought a mini-van and that transformed our lives. He passed his test and we were mobile at last. Shortly after that we did the Partington Men's Club and the concert secretary invited us back to his house for sandwiches. He got his wife up and I don't think she was too pleased, because she had her curlers in. We were chatting until about four in the morning, when we eventually decided it was time to leave – having had a drink or two (this was before the breathalyser was introduced).

As we got in the van Eddie said to me, 'You drive.' I had never had a lesson in my life but he said, 'You've got to start some time; besides I can't do all the driving.' So I said 'Okay', got in, Eddie showed me the basics and off I went. I was a bit shaky to start with but as the morning progressed I improved and quite surprised myself. I drove around Manchester, eventually ending up near the airport, and then Eddie said, 'We'll go home now,' so off we went. We had arrived in an area close to my home when I came to a split in the road like a 'Y' junction.

I turned to Eddie and said, 'Is it up or down?' meaning the indicator.

He said, 'Go straight on,' meaning the road.

Taking his advice, I went straight on and manoeuvred around an obstacle. Eddie then said, 'I think there's a police bike behind us. Now don't worry if he pulls us over, you dive on to the passenger seat and I'll jump out. I'll then go around the back of the van and get into the driver's seat.'

When you've had a few at that time of the morning you think any suggestion is a good idea. So Eddie did just what he said he would. Having watched our antics, the policeman came over and said, 'Do you think I'm *?!*! blind?'

Then he said to me, 'You come here. What's the number of this van?' so Eddie told him. 'I'm not talking to you,' he said, then turning back to me, he said, 'Walk up that white line.' So I walked up the white line and he didn't say when I should stop; I was nearly back in Manchester when he shouted, 'Come back!'

I turned round and all the time I thought about Mum and how to tell her they'd locked me up and thrown away the key. I was sure the outcome of this whole event was going to be really bad news. Poor old Eddie had to drive all the way home, having promised to take his documents into the police station the next day.

When Eddie arrived at the station, the duty officer obviously recognized him and said, 'Hello Eddie, what trouble have you been in then?' Eddie told him about the previous night and he said, 'Let's have a look at the ticket,' so Eddie showed it to him. The officer then walked into a back room. Five minutes later he returned, ripping up the ticket and saying, 'You're all right, Eddie, but don't let it happen again.'

The officer turned out to be a friend that Eddie had met at Main Road football ground.

You can imagine how relieved I was when Eddie came to my house and told me what had happened. Looking back, it was remarkable that we got off so lightly. Mind you, it was four o'clock in the morning, there were no other cars on the road and we didn't do anyone else any harm. Unfortunately, the policeman who let us off is dead now, but he worked at Main Road for many years, operating the security cameras for the matches. I'll always remember him as a nice sort of guy. I wonder why!

After this incident I decided that it was about time I learnt to drive. I ended up having 36 lessons because I was nervous and I struggled with my reversing. Eventually, after all these lessons, I decided I was ready for my test. The test was in a place called Withington and when I arrived the instructor introduced himself. Brief formalities over, he sat next to me in the car and we were ready to start. I thought I was doing all right until I came to a right turn.

For some reason I stopped for ages. I waited until the road was absolutely clear and then the instructor said, 'Mr Mead, are we turning right?'

'Eventually … yes,' I replied.

'That's it,' I thought, 'he's bound to fail me now.' But he didn't, and I passed first time. He did seem concerned about my glasses, though, and pointed out that I should have them checked regularly. I was over the moon; it's a great feeling when you pass your driving test.

I remember the first time I went to Piccadilly, Manchester,

and I was driving along Princess Parkway. I came to some traffic lights and instead of putting the car in first gear, I put it in reverse and hit the car behind me. That was more or less straight after my driving test but, like they say, 'You don't learn to drive until you've passed your test.' I soon discovered that driving is all down to experience and with practice it becomes like a sixth sense. I was quite chuffed because it took Eddie three times to pass his test. To be fair, he probably would have passed the second time but unfortunately an examiner had been killed the day before he took his test. Not surprisingly, Eddie's examiner must have been very nervous and he failed him. (Well, that's Eddie's story!)

My first car was an Austin 1100. This was back in 1965 and I can still remember the registration – CNF 771C. I had many cars after that, but I can never remember their numbers. I think a lot of people can remember their first car. The great thing about mine was that I'd paid for it within 12 months and still had about £500 in the bank! That was after two years of being in show business. Of course, it was downhill from then on...

3

All down to experience

You may have noticed that up until now there'd been a definite lack of girls in my life, although I'd got on very well with them when I was younger. To be honest, I wasn't really bothered about them. I was so immersed in music – it was my guitar that dominated my teenage years. However, I do remember one occasion at the Locarno in Sale when this attractive young lady called Ann took a shine to me. Why she picked on me I'll never know, but I was dead chuffed because a lot of my mates fancied her. Mind you, our courtship only lasted three or four weeks!

I was performing at the Stonemasons at that time, so I decided to impress Ann by inviting her on a gig. I thought she'd like to see me on stage with my guitar – doing my macho bit. In those days everybody smoked and a guy called Tony Gurbett offered me a cigarette. In order to look cool I took one and put it between my lips while Tony fiddled with his gas lighter. He flicked the lighter and the flame went so high that it shot right past my cigarette and caught my nose instead. The biggest blister you've ever seen grew on my nose and I looked like Charlie Carolie the clown. Everybody thought this was funny apart from me. I was so embarrassed because Ann had witnessed everything. It really destroyed my image. Surprisingly, though, she stuck with me even after that.

As well as singing at the Stonemasons, I also performed in a pub called The Ship, close to where my Uncle George and Auntie Joyce lived. One night they agreed to let Ann and I stay with them. We were kissing and cuddling on the sofa when Auntie Joyce came down and said, 'Cyril, that's enough. Go up to bed.' Not surprisingly that put paid to my courtship. Mind you, I discovered later on that Ann had been two-timing me. I couldn't blame her I suppose. I don't think I was much of a catch and she was quite mature for her age. After that experience I went back to the guitar.

The bookings were coming in on a regular basis by then and I remember Eddie and I started doing a place called the College Club. This was in the '60s and it was always quiet on Tuesdays and Thursdays. To draw the crowds the club would organize stag nights and they'd book five comedians and six strippers.

There was only one dressing room at the club and we needed plenty of room to get changed into our collars, dicky bows and the rest of our outfit. Bear in mind that Eddie and I were still teenagers then. We tried not to look at the strippers who shared the room with us and fortunately they didn't seem at all concerned about us. However, because I'm quite short I'd often turn round and find a pair of boobs close to my face, coupled with a strong smell of talcum powder. On one occasion a stripper said to me as she looked at my guitar, 'Is that real mother-of-pearl?' and I just answered, 'Yes, yes,' very quickly, because I was too embarrassed to say any more.

One of the strippers was called Beverley. She was a big, tall, coloured girl, and a laugh a minute, but I don't think she was really cut out for that type of work although she looked the part. In those days Eddie and I could stand at the bar, have a drink and watch all the acts (which was quite a bonus for two teenagers) for nothing. One night we were standing at the bar watching Beverley perform. She wore tassels on her boobs, but when she swung them one fell off, so she picked it up and put it on a chair. When the time came for her to remove her stockings she sat down on the same chair. Unbeknown to her, the tassel got stuck to her bottom. When she stood up again and turned round all the lads started to fall about laughing, but she wasn't fazed; in fact she tried to spin it for them. They responded with a roar of approval. Beverley certainly was a character.

Another stripper was called Kinky Minky. She came from London, and she was a real hard case. She had an aggressive attitude and really ripped into the fellas and they were abusive in return. It didn't seem to bother her.

The following act was a young girl from the Manchester area. I think she was called Rose Marie and she was only about 16 years old. She'd agreed to perform because the owner of the club had goaded her on. He told her what a lovely young girl she was and then suggested she became a stripper. He'd been getting girls from London and they weren't that good, and he must have thought he could save money if he found them himself.

The owner eventually got this girl to do a strip. As she walked onto the stage all the lads were hooting and howling because she was so attractive, but when she started to undress, instead of slinging her stuff all over the place like the others did, she folded everything neatly as if she was getting ready for bed. Well, the lads started to laugh at her, which was a shame because she'd never done this before. Bless her. She got through the first act and when she came on to do her second one Kinky Minky came on half-way through and they started working together.

Luckily, Eddie and I spotted a couple of old comedians, who had seen a lot of this sort of thing before, edging for the door, so we followed them. I won't tell you what was happening on stage, but the compere stopped the performance. The following week it was the cleanest stag show you can imagine, because half the audience were plain-clothes policemen waiting to see a repeat performance!

People always say to us that it must have been tough when we first started performing, but we didn't know what to expect. We thought it was all 'par for the course', as they say. We just assumed that *everyone* worked two or three clubs a night like we did, and we maintained that workload even when we were semi-professional. We got up at seven o'clock in the morning to go to work, did a full day, then rushed home for tea (or dinner as it's called in the south), then it was straight out to the clubs.

At around this time we met up with Bernard Manning. We'd met a guitarist at the Yew Tree and he said to Eddie that Bernard might be able to help us. He had a club in Collyhurst in Manchester and apparently he was always looking for new talent. Eddie and I talked it over as we rehearsed back home in our front room at 4 Moorcroft Road. (We had an upright piano and a set of drums belonging to my younger brother, plus my amp and tape recorder. I wish I'd kept those tapes, because I bet there's some good stuff on them!)

Eddie decided to visit Bernard after rehearsing, so he took the number 50 bus to Piccadilly. During the ride Eddie thought about our fee. 'What can I charge Bernard Manning? I'll charge £100 for the week. That'll be all right.' But by the time he changed to another bus for Collyhurst, he'd got it down to £50.

When he arrived Bernard was standing at the door in his shirt-sleeves and braces and he said to Eddie, 'Can I help you, son?'

Eddie replied, 'I'm Eddie of Syd and Eddie.' We weren't called Little and Large then and we couldn't afford second names!

'Well, can I help you?' said Bernard.

'Yes,' answered Eddie. 'This guitarist from the Yew Tree said you'd give us a job for the week.'

'Oh yes, I've heard of you two. How much do you want?'

Eddie said we wanted £60, Bernard said he would give us £50 and Eddie agreed. So we got the job, but little did we know what this would entail, and besides it was only £25 each. We ended up doing three clubs a night for seven nights (the Embassy, the Palladium and a nightclub in Manchester called the Wilton Club).

Ever since those early days in our career we've always stayed in touch with Bernard. He's a man that you either love or hate and fortunately we always got on well together. I know a lot of people think he's crude, but deep down he's got a heart of gold.

One of his passions is old-age pensioners and he always used to open his club (and I'm sure he still does) in Collyhurst every Tuesday and Thursday for coffee mornings so that they could be entertained. On one occasion, during the introduction of the Poll Tax, there was an old gentleman who had actually been imprisoned in Strangeways for not paying his bill. Moved by the story, Bernard went along and paid the fine so that the man could be released. A lot of people don't know about that story because Bernard didn't want any recognition for it. Apparently Granada TV and the local papers got a tip-off and they all went flocking round to Bernard, but he just told them very politely to go away as he didn't want the attention. Bernard prefers to do his charity work quietly. He's not looking for credit for the things he does.

Later on, when our reputation had grown and we were starting to become well known, I took Sheree (my second wife) to Bernard's club. She'd never been there before and in some ways it was like going into the lion's den. He gave us a lovely table and we made ourselves comfortable. The place was packed because Bernard's club was and still is very popular. He walked on stage and I thought, 'Oh no, I'm going to get it here. I'll be the butt for all his gags,' but he said, 'Right, you lot, there's a local young man in tonight and he's not forgotten his roots; it's Syd Little, and he's sitting over there. Now, I don't want you lot to bother him.' I was nervously waiting for the abuse, but it never came – not a word – he was as good as gold. We had a fantastic night, and Sheree enjoyed it.

But Bernard can be cruel at times. In the Embassy Club there was only one way in and out because there was no stage door. You had to go in the front of the club with whatever equipment you had in order to reach the dressing room. (I remember having to pull my enormous Vox amp through the crowd myself, before I had my brother David as a roadie.) Well, Bernard had a reputation for giving new talent a chance and one agent in particular kept sending him foreign acts. On one occasion there was a German ukulele/banjo player who was okay but not really Embassy and Palladium Club material. He couldn't speak much English, but he went on and did his act, and it was a bit embarrassing because you sensed that the audience didn't like him.

If Bernard didn't like you there'd be no chance of appearing the following night. As this poor German finished his act Bernard came on and had a go at him, and the guy just smiled and said, 'Ya, ya, ya!' because he didn't have a clue what was going on. Eventually Bernard said, 'Look at the poor so and so, he thinks he's coming back tomorrow!' and the guy carried on waving his ukulele on his way out through the crowd. Bernard was still going for him until he disappeared, saying things like, 'I bet you think you're coming back tomorrow, ya, ya, well you're not!'

All the waiters in the clubs were part of Bernard's act and he would have a go at them too, and they would have a go at him. He had quite a double act developed with a Polish guy, but I can't repeat some of the things they used to do. It was very funny, though.

It may seem as if I lived a very unholy life being around all those strip clubs, but Eddie and I didn't know any different. We just took it all in our stride. To us it was simply a way of making a living, and we earned more that way than we did in our day-time jobs – plus the fact that we really enjoyed ourselves. We got a real buzz from performing live on stage and the different audiences made it more of a challenge. One night it would be a stag party with just men, where we'd be well received, and then another night it might be a hen party where the audience's attitude would be completely different.

At this stage the engagement book was nearly full with gigs just around Manchester. We couldn't go far because we didn't have any transport at first. But even when we did eventually get the van, we continued working around Manchester.

With the gigs coming thick and fast, it was inevitable that sooner or later I would have to make the break with my painting work. One day the boss said to me, 'You've got to work overtime tonight.'

'No I can't work overtime, boss,' I replied, 'because I told you I'm doing this gig.'

'Well,' he said, 'you've got to make up your mind whether you want to be a painter and decorator or an entertainer.'

'You've known for a long time that I wanted to do this gig,' I said in return.

'Well, you're going to have to make a choice. If you don't work tonight you can pick up your cards in the morning.'

'Right,' I said, and walked out.

The following day I went to see the boss, George Jones Senior, and he said that my cards weren't ready – could I come back the next day? George Jones Junior came round to my house and he obviously wasn't very pleased.

'Don't throw your apprenticeship away,' he said. 'You've done five years and you've only got one more to go. You know we like you being with us.'

But I just answered him, 'No, it's all right. Your Dad doesn't want me so that's it. I'll get my cards.'

I went round to Eddie's and told him that I'd been sacked. 'Well,' he said, 'you've got to get yourself another job, because we've not got enough in the book yet.'

In actual fact we were quite busy, but by Eddie's standards if there were a couple of nights free that wasn't good enough. It was October so I thought it wouldn't be easy to find another decorating job, and I went back to the Youth Employment Office without much hope. Surprisingly they were able to offer me painting work with a firm called

Fishers & Co. of Chorlton-cum-Hardy. It was a great job because it was supported by a union, which meant it was harder for them to sack you.

I had been there for about a fortnight and was really enjoying myself doing paper-hanging and all sorts of jobs that George wouldn't let me do, when Eddie suddenly said to me one day, 'We're turning pro.'

'Well, okay,' I thought.

Back at work my new boss called me into the office and said, 'I believe you want to leave us.'

'Yes,' I replied, 'I'm going into show business and I'm going to be a professional.' (I'll always remember my Mum saying that I would need a 'proper' job as I wouldn't always be able to rely on show business. How wrong can you be?) The boss didn't make a fuss, but just wished me luck and shook my hand, which I thought was very nice.

Once I'd packed in my job it only remained for Eddie to do the same. So he went to the bosses at Metropolitan Vickers (a big electronics firm in Manchester) to say he was leaving, and they cheered. They cheered because Eddie was never at work. Our show-biz lifestyle was keeping him out late and he had difficulty waking up for work in the mornings. And at Vickers they hadn't been able to sack him because of the strong union.

Once we'd made the break with our day-time work, life was a bit strange all of a sudden. Now we were professionals there was nothing to do during the day. Eddie would come to my house and we'd go into the front room and rehearse songs to improve the act, but we still had the whole day to ourselves. I had my little hobbies which included making plastic model boats, and I'd also try my hand at writing music, and then, of course, there was my guitar. I used to love just sitting and playing.

After a while we teamed up with a lad called Frank Heeley, who used to work for the *Express* newspaper in Manchester. He also worked at night and the three of us would go off to Blackpool for the day.

Eventually Eddie decided that it was time for us to spread our wings a bit and we had to start moving out of Manchester, so we began to look for an agent. We were working in a club in Stockport then, and that's where we met our first managers, Mike Dynan and Ronnie Cryer. Ronnie soon took over the reins from Mike because he was convinced we had something going for us – we were getting rave reviews all over Manchester.

Ronnie invited us to his mum's house in St Annes for Sunday lunch so we could discuss our future together. After a fantastic meal he produced the contract and said, 'Here you are, lads, sign that.'

So we read it and Eddie said, 'Your commission looks a bit steep.' It was about 38 or 48 per cent, as I remember.

'No,' replied Ronnie, 'it's based on a sliding scale. When you're earning that much you'd be giving it to the taxman anyway. Besides, you'll be working for thousands before you reach that stage.'

Well, in no time at all we were giving him 48 per cent because we hadn't read the contract properly. The percentage

was a big chunk out of our wages and we were only earning £75 a week, split between the two of us. Still, there
seemed little we could do just then, so we just left things
for a while.

Sometime after Ronnie became our agent, we were performing at the Old Trafford Working Men's Club in our
own show. I knew we were the stars because our names were
in coloured chalk! (I know that's an old joke, but I couldn't
resist it.) The club had also booked this comedian from
Liverpool, and he really was a cocky so-and-so. He had a
great pair of sideburns and a fabulous Beatle haircut to go
with it. Putting his feet up on a chair, he said straight off,
'I'll go on first because I've got a double.' A 'double' means
that you're appearing somewhere else the same night.

Before the show we had a good chat with this comedian
and he said that we should branch out more and get around
the country. We asked him how we could do that and he
advised us to get a London agent. Then it was his turn to go
on stage and he paralysed them! A couple of weeks later,
Eddie and I were watching the *Royal Variety Show* on TV,
and guess who stole the show? That same comedian who
had appeared with us two weeks before – Jimmy Tarbuck.

Admiring his success, we took his advice and looked out
for a London agent. Coincidentally, we were told soon after
this that one had seen our act at the Garrick Club in Leigh
where we'd been performing. We phoned Ronnie to ask if
the agent had liked us and he said, 'Yes, but he thinks you
were "blue".'

'What do you mean, we were "blue"?'

'He said you were picking your nose on stage and you said the word "bloody",' Ronnie replied. The agent turned out to be Joe Collins, father of that well-known actress, Joan Collins. We agreed to see what he could do for us down south.

Soon after that, however, Eddie and I knew we had to get rid of Ronnie. The percentage he was taking from our wages was crippling. We decided to go to a London solicitor and he asked us what the hell we were doing signing a contract like that. It proved to be a painful lesson and it taught us never to sign a contract with an agent again. In future we would simply work on the basis of a gentleman's agreement. This whole episode was especially difficult for Eddie because he was just about to get married to his first wife. They had been saving up, and now we each had to pay about £300 to get out of our contract with Ronnie. Financially, it wiped us out.

Despite the financial hiccup, however, we were having a great time working around Manchester. Our average day consisted of performing at three clubs a night and then staying at the bar until two o'clock in the morning, followed by a big curry in an Indian restaurant. We'd finally get home at about four o'clock in the morning. I'll always remember how my Dad was into fishing in a big way, and when Eddie dropped me off outside my home, Dad would be sitting on his fishing box waiting for a lift. It was a strange sight to see me going in as he was coming out.

All down to experience

On 30 August 1964 Eddie and I had been professional for nearly a year. We were driving back from Barnsley in Yorkshire that night. The sky was lovely and clear and it was still light when we got home. I noticed our Peter standing at the gate and thought it was strange because Peter was married and he didn't live at home any more. What was he doing at our house at that time in the morning? As I stepped out of the car Peter broke down and told me that Dad had died. I was so shocked. My Dad was only 50 years old and I thought it had to be some kind of a joke. But when I went inside and saw Mum curled up on the settee (the doctor had given her a sedative) I had to believe him.

I asked what had happened and Peter said Dad had been fishing all day at Bridgwater in Somerset. He'd returned with his mates and because he was late, my Mum had left his dinner in the oven. He gobbled the food down, then ran all the way to the Brooklands Trade and Labour Club because he'd missed the bus. Rushing in, he sat down and ordered a pint. When it came, he lifted it up and said, 'I've been waiting for this all day.' Then he just keeled over.

He was taken into the dressing room, and the lads tried to give him the kiss of life, but it was too late. I got the full story later from the group who were appearing at the club, The Nobodies, who we knew well. They were able to say, 'Yes, we were there the night your Dad died,' and told me all about it. They thought he'd swallowed his tongue or something like that, but their attempts to resuscitate him didn't work and he died. He was always saying, when he'd had a few, 'I don't want to linger on, I want to go with a pint in my hand,' and he did. They closed the club for the night out of respect for him.

So that was it – my Dad was dead. Although I owe a lot to my Dad – I wouldn't have learnt to play the guitar if it hadn't been for his encouragement – there were times when you'd have thought it was his career not mine. On one occasion when I had a girlfriend, which was quite rare for me, I remember him returning from the club and poking the fire furiously, saying, 'That's it, now women are in your life that's the end of your career.'

When I think about it now I can see that to some extent my Dad tried to live his life through my career, but I have to say that I was enjoying myself so much that it didn't really bother me. I can also see, looking back, that he was very concerned for me and saw the potential that I had wherever I performed. I could see in his eyes that he was willing me on. I would love for him to have seen me a bit further on in my career, but it wasn't to be.

Understandably, this was a very sad time for our family and it took my Mum a long time to come to terms with Dad's death, especially as he died so young.

Life had to go on, though, and that year Eddie and I started to do what were known as 'rock concerts'. These were concerts where you had four or five major artists appearing together, not like today when you just get one main star as the top of the bill. On one of our first tours we worked with Dionne Warwick, the Searchers, the Isley Brothers and the Zombies. We were billed as the comedy comperes. It was our job to be funny while the groups were setting up backstage.

Well, we decided to put the concerts down to experience because we certainly weren't in it for the money! I think we were paid £75 a week, split between the two of us, for a six-week tour.

Out of that money we had to find and pay for our own digs. We became a running joke with all the lads on the coach because we'd arrive at a city and Eddie and I would jump off and go looking for the cheapest digs. When we got back we'd tell the lads how much they cost and they'd burst out laughing. I think we sometimes managed to find digs for as little as 10s. It was all right for the rest of them – they were at the best hotels in town.

On one of our tours we worked with Gene Pitney, the Rockin' Berries, and Lulu and the Lovers, and we were appearing at the Odeon in Slough. We shared our dressing room with Peter and Gordon, who were the big act of the show, but fortunately they changed at their hotel. One evening Eddie and I were having a shave when there was a knock on the door and Eddie said, 'Come in.'

A young guy popped his head round the door and asked, 'Are Peter and Gordon in here?'

'Yes,' I said, 'but they're getting dressed at the hotel.'

'Well, can I wait in here for them?'

'Yeah, sure,' we said, and carried on shaving. As we glanced at the guy's reflection in our mirror – he was unshaven, hair all over the place, long dark overcoat and holes in his shoes – we looked at each other, and then again at this person, and we realized that sitting in our dressing room was one of the biggest stars of the day. It was none other than Paul McCartney.

Before long, word got round that Paul was in our room, so the rest of the cast including Gene Pitney walked in, and eventually Peter and Gordon arrived. Paul picked up my guitar, turned it around (he's left handed) and started to strum and sing songs from the Beatles' latest album *Rubber Sole*. I can still picture him now doing 'Norwegian Wood'.

Anyway, they asked Paul to announce the opening act of the night, which was Eddie and myself. Somehow I don't think Paul will even remember any of this now. But I'm still the proud owner of that same guitar Paul played all those years ago. It might have a touch of woodworm now, but nothing could persuade me to part with it. Eventually the audience found out that Paul McCartney was in the building and there were as many people waiting outside the stage door as there were watching the show. He managed to get out unscathed, though.

Looking back on those early years, they were good times and we had the opportunity to meet lots of stars, especially at the Liverpool Cabaret Club. In 1964, for instance, we met Ken Dodd. I remember the club manager saying, 'Ken wants to meet you after your show.' Then he went on, 'But I bet he doesn't buy you a drink.' Well, we never expected him to, but the manager said that he was tight and that he wouldn't give a door a bang.

We met Ken and he gave us some great advice. 'Write down everything you do,' he said. 'If you perform a new joke on stage always write it down.' We chatted for about an hour, but I spent most of the time wondering if he would buy us a drink! He never did, by the way, but drink or no drink, I wish we'd taken his advice and written things down.

During the '60s gambling was allowed in the cabaret clubs. One night we were coming into one of these clubs in Liverpool when we discovered a long queue of people waiting to get in. We had to push our way to the front, saying that we were the 'turn' that night. When we got to the front door a bouncer opened the slide hatch and we told him we were the cabaret. He opened up and at that very moment four Chinese gentlemen rushed in behind us. The bouncer let them in because he knew they were good gamblers.

The crowd started shouting because these Chinese had been let in. 'Oi, you've jumped the queue!' they yelled.

'They're the police,' said the bouncer.

Someone in the crowd shouted back, 'But they're Chinese!'

The bouncer, as quick as a flash, replied, 'It's Interpol!' You can't beat the Scouser's sense of humour.

Working mainly in Liverpool, Manchester and the north-east, we had never been out of Britain until the chance came for us to go to France and tour the American bases. This was in the '60s, remember, before Charles de Gaulle kicked them out. We were booked to do quite a few camps, scattered all over France and near the borders of Spain, Holland and Italy. Some of the journeys were horrendous, but like so many episodes in our career, we just put it down to experience.

We arrived in France and the agent told us that we would not be working for a couple of days so if we wanted to have a look round Paris we were free to do so. Eddie and I walked the streets of Paris and we couldn't believe our eyes. We saw the 'ladies of the night', as I call them, just touting for business in broad daylight. We were shocked because everything was so blatant. We'd assumed that our dads were joking when they told us about such things, but now we knew this wasn't true, and everywhere was open 24 hours a day. It was amazing.

After our trip to Paris we drove to a base between France and Holland. We were to perform in front of enlisted men and they were really hard because they didn't want to be there. It was an all-male audience and they had a stripper from Holland as part of the show. As well as being the comperes, Eddie and I had to set up the stage for this stripper. Her set consisted of a sheepskin rug, a little lamp on a table, and a chair. Unlike Kinky Minky, this girl was a real professional and very artistic. Once she'd done her strip, we were to come on, remove the props and carry on with the show.

She did her act, which went down very well (they always did in front of an all-male audience, especially Americans), but when we came off she was in tears. We asked her what the matter was and she said, 'Where are my clothes?' Apparently the lads, the GIs, had taken all her clothes as she removed them, and now she had nothing to wear.

To help her out we went back on stage and said, 'Gentlemen, could you please give the lady her clothes back?' But we just got a load of abuse and they didn't want to know.

Eventually this big sergeant major came on – he was bigger than John Wayne! – and he said, 'Okay you guys, the lady wants her clothes back.' Slowly but surely, he got a response. There'd be a mutter of, 'Oh gee, sarge, we wanted something to remember her by,' and a bra would come over, then a pair of knickers, then a dress, then a nylon stocking, and so on, until eventually everything she owned was thrown back.

They were rough places, though. Some of the stories we heard of how various acts had been treated were horrendous. Fortunately they seemed to feel sorry for us, especially me, because Eddie was always ribbing me. We also went down well because at that time 'Mule skinner blues' was one of our big numbers and the Americans loved it. Because they appreciated country-and-western music so much, it brought the house down and saved our bacon. I have to say that touring the bases wasn't an enjoyable experience, but at least it was work.

You may like to know how we ended up with the stage names of 'Little and Large'. Originally we were going to clubs around Manchester and the north-east just as 'Syd and Eddie'. The names seemed fine to us and the people we knew were quite happy, but when we started to move around the country some of our clients didn't share that opinion. Joe Collins started to book us into little restaurants and cabaret rooms in the south and we did one place in Lewes, near Brighton. The owner said he wanted us back, but our names had to be changed.

We asked Joe why and he said, 'Look at it this way. If I go to a club owner and say, "I've got this great act; they sing, they dance, they do comedy," he may say, "What are they called?" and I could say, "Fred and Charlie." '

We got the message! At that time we were in Sunderland doing our usual fortnightly stint up there, and Eddie went to a second-hand shop and got hold of an old typewriter. One night after the show he went up to his bedroom and typed all through the night. The next morning he appeared all bleary eyed with a long list of possible names. With Eddie being very sporty and liking football and golf, the list was full of names like 'Syd and Eddie Nicklaus' or 'Syd and Eddie Summers'. You had Mike and Bernie Winters, so Eddie thought we could have something similar.

But right in the middle of this long list was 'Little and Large'. I turned to Eddie and said, 'That's it, Little and Large.'

'Yes,' said Eddie, 'that's the one I picked too.'

So that day our new stage names were born.

4

Brotherly love

It was during 1964 while I was still living at home with Mum and the twins, Linda and David, that I met Mavis, who was to become my first wife. Mavis was Linda's best friend. We'd been courting for about two months when Eddie and I were offered the chance to do our first summer season.

It was a very cold February night and we were working in a club called The Castaways in Birmingham. It was a fabulous place, all decked out like a desert island with a big shipwreck and palm trees. The effect was so realistic that you felt like a genuine castaway even though you were in the middle of Birmingham!

We were enjoying a great week when a gentleman called Billy Forest came in to see us. Most people on the club circuit knew Billy because he was a well-known agent for the Channel Islands and booked all the summer shows out there. At this stage in our careers we'd reached a point where our money wasn't too bad and I think he knew this. After watching our performance Billy suggested we got together for a chat. As we talked he told us in his broad Brummy accent that if we wanted he could offer us a season in Jersey at a place called the Sunshine Hotel. The season would run for 22 weeks and we were allowed to take our families and treat it like a holiday.

Sitting in Birmingham in the middle of February, this sounded like a very attractive deal. There wasn't much money on offer, but because Eddie and I could use it as a bit of a holiday we agreed to go. Mavis wasn't very happy about this, but the local shoe shop she worked for had a branch in Jersey, so they arranged for her to have a transfer during the summer. Looking back, I think that if I'd gone on my own we would never have ended up getting married, but that wasn't the way it turned out.

Billy had said there wasn't much money in this deal and we soon discovered how right he was. In order to try and ease things a little Eddie and his first wife Sandra, and myself and Mavis all decided to share the same house. On reflection this wasn't a good idea because Mavis and Sandra didn't really hit it off. Sandra was unhappy because Mavis was working at the shoe shop and she felt that she'd been lumbered with all the cooking and housework. I suppose she did have a point. Anyway, towards the end of the season we ended up just tolerating each other and making the best of it. Ideally, we should have had places of our own because we were there for such a long time, but we simply couldn't afford it.

Work-wise, however, it was a good summer and the show was great. We worked with a comedian called Sonny Jones and a fabulous double act called McNeil and Trotter. All three were older than Eddie and myself, but they were very good acts and really funny.

During the day I didn't have much to do. Eddie was either playing golf or out with Sandra, and Mavis was at work, so I was on my own most of the time. I remember going down to the beach at St Oens. Bored with being on my own, I enrolled for some scuba diving lessons with a local club. I had two or three lessons off this guy and I really enjoyed myself. I was decked out with the old face mask, aqua-lung and flippers, and I was doing quite well.

One day I went down for a lesson and the instructor was busy with a couple of newcomers. While he was teaching them the ropes he said to me, 'Get your gear on, Syd, and just swim round and keep the jetty in view.'

Having tested my gear, I put it on and did as he said. I caught sight of an anchor after a while and thought, 'Oh, that's interesting,' and went to have a look. Then off I went and followed a fish, and spent some time just swimming around happily. Because I'd been distracted by the fish I couldn't see the slipway, but I wasn't worried because I was having such a good time looking for other things on the sea bed. Being light I had a 14-pound lead weight round my waist, but I found I had to keep pushing myself up off the sea bed because the water pressure was holding me down.

Then, quite unexpectedly, I felt this bang on my back and I looked up and saw a little figure paddling above me towards the daylight. I realized that this was my instructor. He came down to me again with just a snorkel and indicated that I should go back to the surface of the water. Following behind him I remember thinking, 'Wow, it seems miles to the surface.' I eventually got there and he guided me back to the beach, which was packed with holiday-makers.

No sooner had we reached the beach than he started to tear me off a strip. He shouted in a way I'd never been spoken to before and I felt like a little boy. What I hadn't known was that I'd been on my way out to sea and I was in 40 or 50 foot of water. I'd probably still be swimming today if he hadn't stopped me. After a short while the instructor calmed down and I carried on with my lessons. And despite my dangerous search for adventure underwater I continued to enjoy diving.

I remember sitting on the beach after my performance in the sea, watching this lad who was in another group. He was doing the same course as me, but when he was swimming around his aqua-lung never went below the waves. He was like that for at least half an hour and all I could see was this aqua-lung going round and round on top of the water. Eventually he came out and walked up to me. 'Syd,' he said, 'it's a whole new world down there!'

'Well,' I thought, 'how would you know?'

The funny thing is that although I took diving lessons and could cope under the water, I was hopeless at swimming on top of it. I don't like going out of my depth and can only seem to swim for short distances.

One day I was sitting on the beach doing some writing.

All of a sudden I heard a girl screaming, 'Help! Help!' I instinctively ran into the water to rescue her and only then thought, 'What am I doing? I can't really swim!' I was going towards her and I suddenly realized that I could just balance on my toes in the sand. I didn't want to swim because I thought I might get into trouble myself and be no use to the girl. So with one toe in the sand I managed to grab the girl and pull her onto the beach. Believe it or not, I actually saved her life. Later her parents thanked me and I thought, 'If only they knew that I still had my toe stuck in the sand.' But I didn't tell them!

One day in June, Mavis gave me a bit of a shock. She told me that she'd been to the doctor and discovered she was pregnant. When he told her that the baby was due in February we knew we had to get things moving. We told our parents and made arrangements to go back to Manchester and get married. We had to find someone to cover for us at the show during this period. Everything seemed to happen so quickly: we arrived in Manchester, got married, and then went straight back to Jersey to finish the season.

When we finally left Jersey at the end of the summer, I think our cars were rather glad to get off the island. We seemed to have spent the entire time in third gear. Don't get me wrong, though; it's a lovely part of the world, even if it *is* possible to see it all in a week. Having said that, I'd go back any day. At the time, however, we were just happy to be back at home after 22 weeks. Mavis and I settled into a flat in Sale.

In those days the north-east became our second home and we'd do two weeks in Manchester followed by two weeks in the Sunderland area. When you're a singer it's easy to 'follow yourself' and divide your act into several parts. In the clubs you'd often find them doing four or five half-hour spots, say before and after each bingo session. After following this format ourselves quite a few times Eddie and I got really fed up, because with comedy you can't work in the same way. You tend to do your best spot first, to get you off the ground, and then you have to follow it with more average material. When you've done this four or five times, you haven't got much left and we often ended up singing songs.

We thought this was silly, really, because in our eyes the audience wasn't getting value for money. So we came up with an idea and told our agent that we weren't going up to Sunderland any more unless we could do just two half-hour spots in the clubs. We pointed out that our revised routine would offer the audience good value. After listening to our argument he agreed to our proposal and said things would be put in motion.

We had agreed to do a 'noon and a night' at Sunderland – that's a Sunday noon show and an evening one in the same place. We went on at noon as planned and did our two spots. Time is obviously a bit limited at the lunch break, so the two spots felt great. We went back in the evening and while I was putting the amplifier on the stage (we didn't have a road manager then) I noticed that the place was packed. I also saw that the men who'd been at the lunch-time show had obviously enjoyed it, because they'd returned with their wives.

Brotherly love

Backstage the concert secretary came in and said, 'Right bonny lads, you do one spot now, then we'll have bingo, then you'll do another spot, then we'll have the raffle, and then we'll give you another spot.'

'Whoa, whoa, whoa,' said Eddie, 'hang on, we've told the agent that we're only doing two spots.'

'Well, he never told *me* that, bonny lads,' replied the concert secretary.

'That's what we told the agent,' I chipped in. 'We're only doing two half-hour spots.'

He didn't like this at all and he went up to the committee room, which was halfway up the hall, and obviously told the other members. The next thing we knew, Eddie was summoned to the committee room. He went in and they started to tell him, in no uncertain terms, that we'd got to do more than two spots.

One of them piped up, 'I had to work down the pit for one week to earn what you're getting tonight.'

They really gave him a hard time, but Eddie stuck to his guns and said, 'No, that's it, we're only doing two spots.'

After that he came marching back to me in the dressing room and said, 'Right Syd, that's it, we're not going on, they want more than two spots. Get the amp off the stage.'

From the time that Eddie had walked down the hall back to the dressing room the buzz had gone round that we weren't going on. When I went on stage to remove the amplifier and my guitar, they were booing and throwing beer mats at me. But in the end we won.

The next day we told the agent, 'Look, we thought we told you that we were only doing two spots.'

He turned round and said, 'Well, I thought that if you did three 20-minute spots...' and we thought, 'Oh no, what are we dealing with here?' He just didn't seem to realize what we were getting at. We weren't trying to be awkward – we simply didn't want to spread our act out like that. In the end it was all resolved and we did just the two half-hour spots in the working men's clubs, thank goodness!

While I was researching this book I found a rhyme written on the wall of a working men's club. I thought it would be appropriate to put it in, bearing in mind that a lot of you are familiar with these places. The words are so true, especially if you're an entertainer and have first-hand experience of the clubs. I hope you find it amusing. It goes like this:

You found the Club, arrived on time,
Con. Sec. greets you, all is fine.
Dressing room next to stage, Bingo goes on for an age.
You change your suit, sort out your dots,
Con. Sec. says, 'I want five spots.
They like old ballads here, nothing mod.
I was first in't North to book Ken Dodd.
Here's our duo, best in't land,
Drummer played in colliery band.
Our organist is Tommy Speed,
Real good player but cannot read.
Bingo's finished, half audience has gone,
Ready lads, I'll put thee on.

Give order now for Syd and Eddie,
Pies and pasties now on sale,
Get them when you're ready.'
You try your best, the mike is bad,
The backing is the worst you've had.
The audience applaud them rapturously,
Your turn, more ballads you try in vain,
Con. Sec., 'Don't go on again.
They don't like you lads, your style is wrong,
You only know one kind of song.
All of them old ballads, nothing mod.
I was first in't North to book Ken Dodd.'
You're driving home, feeling sad,
But can things really be that bad?
You've got show business in your bones
And let's face it, some folks don't like Tom Jones.

If you're not familiar with the term 'Con. Sec.', by the way,
it's short for Concert Secretary, and 'dots' refers to music.

One of the main advantages of performing in the north-east
is that the people know how to enjoy themselves. Even today
the working men's clubs stage a show nearly every night of
the week and they can usually offer a good act. I think their
thirst for entertainment must be down to all that Viking
blood!

I remember one nightclub we went to in Middlesbrough
that was thought to be very respectable. We'd been offered a
week's booking and we arrived on the Monday to discover it

was 'Crazy Night'. For this particular evening members of the audience were allowed on stage to do stupid things like drinking a pint and sticking the beer glass on their head or having an egg fight. As you can imagine, the stage was full of spilt drinks and broken eggs, etc. It was a really rough evening!

We did our cabaret act between midnight and one o'clock and we really struggled. When we came off the stage that Monday night, the manager said, 'All right bonny lads?' and we said, 'Well, we struggled there.'

'No, you did well tonight lads, you did well.'

'If that's doing well!' we thought.

Tuesday night came round and it was a stag night. There were five comics and five strippers. When the girls came on all the fellows were shouting, 'Get 'em off!' and swearing and everything. We went on between midnight and one o'clock and again, in our eyes, we really had problems.

Backstage we saw the manager and he asked, 'How was it tonight lads?'

'Oh, we've struggled again, it was really hard work.'

'No,' he said, 'you really did quite well.'

Wednesday night came and it was 'Bierkeller' night so you can imagine what it was like. They were having all these stupid beer games and they were all sloshed. On we went again at the same time and we felt we were still struggling.

As we left the stage with our heads in our hands the manager asked us again, 'How was it tonight lads?'

We answered as usual, 'Oh, we struggled tonight.'

'No,' he said, 'you did great tonight, lads. Thursday, Friday and Saturday are the rough nights!'

This was proving to be a very busy period in our lives. For some time we worked all over the country doing two or three clubs a night, seven days a week. But I think it was during 1969 that Eddie started to get fed up because we didn't seem to be progressing in our careers. On top of that, I think people started whispering in his ear that he could do it on his own and he didn't really need me. They said this because they didn't understand the point of the act or the reason we worked like we did, which meant I said very little. In the early days I don't think I spoke for the first 10 minutes of our act – I perhaps just sang one or two songs, though in time my act did develop more. The thing was that people were missing the whole point: if we'd been the same as Mike and Bernie Winters or Morecambe and Wise, we wouldn't have got anywhere. Our act was different from theirs and that's why people liked us.

Anyway, after all this talk, Eddie said that he wanted us to split, so I didn't stand in his way and said, 'Okay, if that's what you want.'

We had a lot of bookings so we agreed to honour them – we couldn't just say, 'That's it, we've split.' One of these bookings was up in Sunderland and we were doubling with Hartlepool and Newcastle at the time. We'd done the Hartlepool Working Men's Club and were driving along the A19, through Sunderland, when I noticed a car belting along a side road. I realized that it wasn't going to stop at the 'Halt' sign and it was heading straight for us. There was nothing I could do.

I tried to brake, but it was too late, and before I knew it the car had ploughed into the side of us. Our car spun round, hit a bollard, and for a few seconds I was out cold. The next thing I knew, two guys were sticking me on a wall and Eddie was frantically getting our PA system (our amplifier and so on) out of the boot of the car. Then I heard somebody shouting, 'It's going to catch fire!' A bit later I was put in an ambulance and taken to Sunderland General Hospital.

I stayed in the hospital for the next few days having X-rays and tests. Luckily there were no bones broken and I needed just a few stitches in my knees and one eyelid. Eddie, believe it or not, came out unscathed, but when I eventually got out of the hospital a couple of days later, I was on crutches. It seemed like every bone in my body ached.

The garage owner who had towed my car away to a scrapyard said it was a complete wreck, and commented on how lucky we were to be alive. We went to see the wreck for ourselves. Eddie told me later that he'd been slung out of the car (this was in the days before it was compulsory to wear seatbelts), which was quite fortunate because the door had actually shut tight behind him. There was a big bulge in the door where Eddie had been thrown against it and you couldn't get it open. Looking at the damage it was amazing that we both survived.

While I was recovering, our agent asked Eddie if he'd finish the week on his own. This meant he had to do the Wednesday, Thursday, Friday and Saturday performances. He agreed to do the working men's clubs but not the nightclubs. Eddie took me to Newcastle, because I didn't see the point in staying around, and helped me onto the train with all my baggage. He even gave me a *Playboy* magazine to read, but I ached so much I wasn't able to open the pages to look at the pictures! When I finally arrived back in Manchester I was just grateful to get into my own bed.

The following Sunday Eddie came and sat on the side of my bed and we had a little chat. Pulling the money he'd earned that week out of his pocket, he chose to give me half. I've never forgotten that incident – he didn't have to give me the money because I hadn't finished the week. Mind you, after his act of generosity I had to sit there for another hour while he told me how well he'd done on his own! For the time being, though, nothing more was said about splitting up.

It was about this time that Cyril Gibbons died. He was Joe Collins' right-hand man and had been looking after us. Cyril used to be a performer and he'd been on the stage in the '20s, working as a magician and calling himself 'The Great Soraldo'. He was a lovely old gentleman and he liked to be treated with a bit of respect.

I remember being on a tour once with P.J. Proby, who was a big rock star in the '60s – a one-off, really, who dressed in the Tom Jones fashion: long hair in a ponytail (before ponytails were in fashion), big fluffy shirts and buckled shoes. He had a great act, but he was a bit of a boozer and I think he had a self-destruct button. Sadly, his career didn't last that long, although I think at the moment he's making a bit of a comeback. At this time of his career, when we were on his show, he'd split his trousers on stage and all the big venues had banned him. We ended up performing in these horrible, big halls that weren't very good.

One night Cyril came to see us at the Guildford Town Hall. It was a massive place, and we were standing chatting just at the bottom of the stairs by the dressing rooms. Suddenly P.J. Proby walked in through the doors and spat on the floor right by Cyril, who then said, 'Young man, there's a place for that sort of thing.' P.J. just gave him a look as if to say, 'So what!'

Cyril was not impressed with this kind of behaviour because he belonged to a different generation of performers. Even with Eddie and myself he wanted to groom us into an old-time double act, but we just stuck to our guns. We felt that what we were doing was right.

Although we were on his books, we didn't see much of Joe Collins because he was semi-retired. But I do remember that we went to see him in London a couple of times and he took us to watch an Arsenal match – his favourite team. It's funny the things that stick in your mind about people. I remember him telling us that you should never put milk in your coffee if you're having red meat! When we went round to his flat after the match there were pictures of his daughter Joan Collins and her husband Anthony Newley all over the place. I think they must still have been married at that time. It was nice to think that Joe was a genuine family man.

Our workload was still increasing and we started to think about getting a road manager. A road manager is supposed to drive you and all the gear around and set up on stage.

Eddie thought we'd look more professional if we had one. When we'd used the front room at 4 Moorcroft Road for rehearsals, my brother David used to clean Eddie's mini-van. I think he paid him 2s. 6d. So now our thoughts turned to Dave because he was a trained mechanic and could be useful to have around. Incidentally, it's funny how we can hold onto habits going back to our childhood, and Dave would always suck his thumb. Even when he worked in the garage, his hands would be black and his thumb pure white – but he kicked the habit shortly after that.

Our Dave always was and still is a real character. I think if he'd had the opportunity to swap places with me he would have done, because he loves a joke. He was always very talented – what we call 'a meady trait', which means someone who loves being the centre of attention. If he can make people laugh it gives him a buzz, which is what being a comedian is all about. The only trouble with Dave (I'm sure he won't mind me saying this) is his lack of discipline. No matter what people say about comedy and being on stage, you've got to have discipline. A performance might look ad lib, or off the wall, but it still needs self-control, and Dave didn't have that. He would just get carried away and the discipline wasn't there.

His talents included playing the drums and doing impressions. He does a great impression of Max Wall. I remember one occasion a few years after he'd joined us (he started as our road manager in 1971), when we had to get him into Equity because we wanted him on our TV show. We'd done a routine for Equity in Stoke before, and we were appearing at Jollies there, so we asked this Equity rep. to come and see our Dave, hoping he would get a card. He said, 'Okay, I'll come and have a look at him.'

Well, all Dave did then was his Max Wall impression, and we thought that they wouldn't give him an Equity card for just one turn. He'd have to do more than that. So we asked him if he could do anything else, and he said, 'Oh, I can do Norman Wisdom,' so we said that was okay.

On this particular night we started our act and it came to the part where Eddie said, 'I'm not the impressionist, Syd's the impressionist. What are you going to do, Syd?'

So I replied, 'Okay, I'll do one for you,' and walked off the stage.

Dave (who resembles me) came straight on dressed as Max Wall, wearing the tights, balding wig, etc., and he did a superb impression. He did a few funny walks, then left the stage and I came back on immediately. I don't know if the audience was really that gullible, but they just applauded! Did they really think I could have done such a quick change? I suppose with the advent of television they might have thought anything was possible.

Anyway, the routine went down well and when Eddie asked the audience if they liked it they shouted 'Yes!' He asked them if they wanted to see another one and back came the answer 'Yes!' So off I went again and Dave, who'd got changed into his second outfit, walked on doing a Norman Wisdom impression, leaping in the air with his hands in his pockets. Unbeknown to Dave, though, there was a split in the stage and it was about two inches higher at one point.

All of a sudden he fell down. The fall obviously winded him, but he managed to get up, finish his performance and walk off to a round of applause.

I came back on stage and Eddie and I finished the act, but we were worried to death about Dave. When we returned to our dressing room we found him looking ghastly. His face was all white, with yellow blotches on top.

'Dave,' we said, 'you look terrible! What's the matter? You've got blotches all over your face!' It was then we discovered that, trying to be professional, he'd used my make-up but hadn't applied it correctly. Now we knew why he looked so weird! He did get his Equity card, though, and was able to appear on one of our TV shows.

Dave took care of us as our road manager for about 12 years. All three of us would travel up to Sunderland and the north-east and find digs for about £9 a week. This included your bed, breakfast, evening meal and a supper when you came in. It was such a bonus to have hot food after a late-night performance. There was always something left in the oven at the guesthouse because no one took more than their fair share, even though there were 12 or 14 acts staying in the digs. The owners would have gone to bed, but the other acts wouldn't pinch all the food. You could have your breakfast at midday if you wished, too, so £9 for the week wasn't bad.

Our Dave used to come up with us and we'd sit around at breakfast-time chatting to one of the pop groups who were staying at the house. We were the laughing stock for the first few months because they'd ask, 'Where are you tonight?'

Eddie or I would say, 'The other side of Newcastle. I'm not looking forward to that drive.'

'Oh. Isn't your roadie driving, then?' they'd ask.

And we'd say, 'Oh no, he can't drive.'

Well it was like a Styx cartoon: they'd all be laughing because we'd got a roadie who couldn't drive. To be fair, Dave did put the gear on stage and he gave us a better image because with a roadie we appeared to be more professional. Eventually he passed his test and then we enjoyed being chauffeured around.

On one occasion in the '70s, when we were up in Scarborough for the summer season, Dave drove us to a party at a place called Scalby Manor. There was Eddie, Patsy and Sheree (our second wives) and me. We had a great time that evening, but I think our Dave had been drinking. When we got back to the car and headed off to Scarborough he was a bit reckless – and when he started going near the kerb and nearly hitting it, I told him to concentrate and drive better.

He just turned round and told me that I could drive if I thought I could do any better. 'But you're our roadie,' I said.

'What's that got to do with it?' he replied.

As we started to make a name for ourselves we were invited to perform at the Palladium Club in Manchester, and one night there were about three or four big agents who came to watch the show. After the performance they came backstage to see us. Now the problem was that whatever Eddie said, Dave would do, but if I said anything, being my brother, he wouldn't be so keen. This was acceptable with people who knew we were brothers, of course, but it wasn't right in front of these agents.

Well, I turned to Dave and asked him, 'Would you go and get some tea for these gentlemen, please?'

'Get it yourself!' he said.

You should have seen the look on their faces. They were obviously thinking, 'That's weird – the roadie's telling the boss off!' Then Eddie explained that Dave was my brother and I think they understood.

Dave was particularly clever with his hands and he used to make our props. He made Eddie a fantastic Star-burst guitar and a huge Honey Monster. Do you remember the advert where this monster would come on promoting Sugar Puffs? Dave made us an enormous replica, and when we used it on TV we got ourselves into trouble because it was so lifelike. The Kelloggs people told us in no uncertain terms not to do it again.

On another occasion we were in pantomime in Wolverhampton. In those days we weren't actually topping the bill, so Eddie and I shared a dressing room. We went in and I said, 'Right, this is my space,' and Eddie said, 'And this is mine.'

Turning to Dave, he asked, 'Where are we going to put the TV then?'

'We'll put it there,' replied Dave.

But I said, 'No, that's where I need to put my make-up and gear.'

'Well, we'll put it here,' suggested Dave.

But Eddie said, 'No you can't, my stuff's going there.'

Eventually Dave said, 'I know what, I'll build a shelf.'

So he built this shelf in the corner, and it was brilliant. That was back in 1974 and I think it was there until a few years ago. All the stage-hands came in to see this shelf and how solid it was; Dave even sat on it to demonstrate its strength.

This all happened during the winter and on that particular night it was pouring with rain. While we were rehearsing Dave went off to find a TV. When he came back he said that he'd found one in a shop in the town but they wanted a deposit and he needed to know what size screen we preferred. We wrote out the amount for the cheque and told him we wanted a 21-inch screen.

About 20 minutes later he came back again and this time he was soaking wet. 'Do you want a colour TV?' he asked.

'Yes,' we said and off he went again. Then he came back a third time with an agreement that we had to sign. Finally he completed all his errands and, wet through, he sat down.

So we asked him, 'Did you get the telly?'

'Yes.'

'Is it colour?'

'Yes.'

'21-inch?'

'Yes.'

'Well, what's the matter then?'

Dave looked at us sadly and replied, 'It's on ... legs!'

Fortunately this didn't bother him for long. He took the legs off, put the TV on the shelf, and the legs became part of a fantastic coffee table in my Mum's house. Like the shelf in the dressing room, the table was around for years.

Brotherly love

As I've said, Dave was with us for around 12 years. Towards the end I think it got a bit much for him because he was married to Lindy by then and had three children – Louisa, Richard and Claire, his step-daughter – and they lived in Poole in Dorset. With him living in Poole, me living in Preston and Eddie in Bristol, there was a great deal of driving for him to do. In the end Dave decided to call it a day, but I think deep down he still yearns after the show-biz way of life.

5

Angel eyes

Sometime after the car accident which put me in hospital Eddie changed his mind about going solo. He decided that we wouldn't split up. 'We'll just carry on as normal,' he said.

It was during this period of our lives that we first met Major Brian Hart. Brian was a real Major – he used to be in the army and he'd been employed to book the entertainers for the troops in Germany. When he left he decided to use his experience to become an agent on Civvy Street. Brian gave Eddie and me a call. Would we be interested in letting him manage us? As he had a reputation for being a bit of a 'go-getter', we decided to part with Joe Collins and take a chance with Brian.

One of the first shows Brian wanted us to appear on was *Opportunity Knocks*, but this baffled Eddie and me. *Opportunity Knocks* was created for newcomers and we'd been going for eight years! Brian explained that the show was a quick way to get exposure on TV. In the end we agreed to go on but said we didn't want to do an audition. To be honest, we felt that an audition was a bit degrading at this stage in our careers.

So, with our approval, Brian kept pestering the producer Roy Mayoh. I have to add here that everything that happened after *Opportunity Knocks* was down to Roy. He was the man who made us a household name. Anyway, Brian knew that we wouldn't do the audition and Roy kept insisting that we had to. Realizing that we were appearing at the Wooky Hollow in Liverpool (which is where the auditions were being held), Brian persuaded Roy to see us doing a show. Flanked by a couple of people from his team (because they need three for an audition), he called in.

Unbeknown to us, Roy had actually seen our act a few years before at a pub in Manchester and hadn't thought much of it, but this time he was so knocked out that he gave us a chance on his show. For some reason people seem to think that we won *Opportunity Knocks* several times when in fact it was only once. On the second occasion we were beaten by a girl called Glynis Fleetwood. So in two of the three talent competitions we did, we were beaten by girls – first on the Isle of Man, when we were beaten by a 14-year-old girl singing the 'Nuns' Chorus', and then on *Opportunity Knocks* by Glynis singing 'The Lord's Prayer'.

After our first appearance on the talent show Roy tried hard to keep us in the limelight. He gave us spots on the *All Winners' Shows* and guest spots with favourite TV stars like David Nixon on his *Magic Show*. David was a lovely man and it was a thrill to meet him. He was a megastar in his day and in the '70s he was Britain's best-known magician. Do you remember his sidekick, Ali Bongo, who used to help him with all the tricks?

David had a down-to-earth manner and he wasn't at all superior with newcomers like Eddie and me. He was so encouraging to work with because, although he was famous, he made us feel relaxed. Ali would think up the tricks that we were going to do and we couldn't believe how simple they were. He'd have us sitting on a cushion and it would move all over the place, but it was so easily put together (I'm not going to give any secrets away!). Surely, we thought, the audience would realize how it was done – but whether they did or not, I don't think they wanted anyone to show them and spoil the illusion.

After one of the shows – it must have been the last show in the series – we were invited to David's house for a drink. It was a beautiful place in Surrey with an indoor swimming pool and all the little luxuries that make life comfortable. David took a real pride in showing us around, because apparently he'd done a lot of the work himself. He'd dug out the indoor swimming pool and even built a sauna. He was obviously a bit of a DIY enthusiast. The whole experience was certainly a night to remember.

A couple of years later Roy got the chance for us to do a pilot show for a sitcom on TV called *Three in a Bed*, which was about two darts teams. The storyline was built around two pubs. Eddie and I were in the team based in a down-and-out sort of pub, where the landlord was struggling to make money, while the other team in the pub across the road had strippers and the place was packed. The opposing team challenged us to a darts match and this was where all the dialogue came in. The great thing about the show was that we got to know some fantastic actors and actresses, people we'd never come across before, and just like David Nixon, they were warm and friendly towards us even though we were new at the game.

To be honest we're not actors, we're 'red-nose comics', and even when the cast realized how inexperienced we were they still treated us really well. There was Roy Barraclough, who as you know plays Alec Gilroy in *Coronation Street*, and an actor called Norman Chapel, who wasn't quite so well known, and Jackie Clark. The list could go on and on, but all of them really helped us. Working with all these famous stars so early on in our career was good grounding for the fame that lay ahead of us. Out of curiosity I'd like to see our performance on *Three in a Bed* again. I'm sure someone somewhere must have a copy of it.

We were still performing in the clubs, and during one show Brian Jones from the BBC came to see us. Brian was one of the producers for a new series of the popular children's programme *Crackerjack* – hands up all those who used to shout 'Crackerjack!' in their younger days... Well, he liked our act and decided to book us for a 13-week slot on the show. We were to appear with Stuart Sherwin, Michael Aspel and a young lady called Elaine Paige. Like us, Elaine was just starting out on her road to fame. I clearly remember that she was very quiet then, and smelt of chips. I think in those days she lived in a bedsit, but I bet she doesn't now! She was another performer we enjoyed working with and we've met up several times since those early days on *Crackerjack*.

In his enthusiasm to get our career moving, Brian Hart agreed to our TV work but had forgotten all about our club engagements. We had to fulfil our commitments to the Wakefield Theatre Club, The Jolly, Stoke-on-Trent, and lots of others. Most of them were in the north of England. Brian couldn't get us out of the contracts, so for 13 weeks we travelled from Manchester to London and back, every day. We were getting in at four o'clock in the morning, then having to get up again at six for the London train. It was murder.

I think that if we'd agreed to one more week's work we might have had a breakdown. I can remember getting towards the end of the 13th week and sitting on the train going back to Manchester, staring into the houses as the train whizzed past. I was imagining all these people having their dinner and watching *Coronation Street*, and thinking to myself, 'If only I could be there.' It really was a hard time, but it taught us that you should never mix cabaret clubs and TV shows. Physically and mentally it can't be done.

At one of the clubs, the Wakefield, the compere was also in charge of booking the acts. We'd taken on the *Crackerjack* series after we'd started at the Wakefield and one of the TV recordings clashed with a time when we were meant to be at the club. The compere wouldn't let us out of the contract. For some reason he had it in for Brian because in the past he'd messed up and he didn't want to let him off the hook this time. Anyway, the outcome was that we were committed to both shows. We'd started on the Sunday and agreed to do the full week. On the Tuesday there was no way we could make this schedule work. We had to record *Crackerjack* on Tuesday at five o'clock in the afternoon and it was impossible to reach Wakefield in time for our spot. But still the compere insisted that we fulfilled our contract, and he threatened that if we didn't show up he'd sue us.

Naturally, this was quite worrying! So we arranged to get a small plane from Heathrow up to Leeds and then a taxi to Wakefield. Now Brian being Brian, he was trying to get publicity out of every situation and he wanted us to go from Shepherd's Bush Theatre to the airport in our outfits (I was dressed as a toy soldier and Eddie as a tatty ballerina), but we said, 'No way!'

So we got out of that one, and took the plane from Heathrow to Leeds. By the time we started our flight that evening, we were really shattered. Eddie was in the back crashed out and I was in the co-pilot's seat. I don't normally enjoy flying, but this one wasn't too bad because the plane was so small it felt more like a car. As we approached Leeds airport the pilot told me that it was fog-bound but we would still try to land. Because of the fog we had to fly blind down towards the runway and at 200 feet, if we couldn't see it, we had to go back up and try again – three attempts at landing were allowed.

At the first attempt we started to descend and the pilot was asking me if I could see the runway. 'No, I can't see it,' I said. We went lower and lower and I said, 'No, I still can't see it,' then up we zoomed again. We tried to land three times and we couldn't do it. The pilot said we'd have to divert to Manchester airport, so off we went over the Pennines.

He contacted the people at Leeds airport on the radio to tell the taxi driver we wouldn't be landing there. Then he arranged for another taxi to pick us up at Manchester airport, where we had quite a good landing because it was as clear as a bell. We were just about to get into the taxi when Eddie decided to telephone the Wakefield Theatre Club. He spoke to the compere and told him we'd just landed at Manchester airport and that we should arrive in about an hour.

'Don't worry lads,' the compere replied. 'You made the effort, so just have the night off.'

Eddie and I just collapsed in a heap at the airport and wondered why he'd caused such a fuss about us getting there in the first place. It was obvious that he had it in for Brian and not for us, but it would have made life so much easier if they'd sorted out their differences before we went through all that drama.

Although it was TV work, *Crackerjack* nearly ruined our career. For the next 18 months we had to try to get rid of the image that the series had created and establish ourselves with an older audience again. We simply didn't want to be identified as kids' entertainers. After *Crackerjack* we'd turn up at working men's clubs and they'd be full of kids – you'd see them in the front row, with milk bottles placed alongside their parents' pints of Guinness. We've got nothing against children, but we didn't slog round all the rough clubs for 12 years to end up performing for them. Maybe if Brian had thought things through a bit more he would have refused the *Crackerjack* work, but at least it did mean we were appearing on TV.

After *Crackerjack*, Brian thought it was about time we had a 'proper' London agent again (Brian being based in the Midlands, we'd not been directly represented in London for a while), and eventually Michael Grade agreed to take us on. Although he wasn't our agent for long he did get us in with the big boys in London. As you probably know, Michael moved on to bigger things such as Channel 4 and Controller of BBC Entertainment, then First Leisure.

Before he left us Michael handed us over to Norman Murray. Norman was a completely different kettle of fish – a hard-nosed London agent who didn't endear himself to some people. In fact, a lot of people found him very hard to get on with and he was very outspoken. There was definitely a clash of personalities between him and Brian and I think they only just tolerated each other. In time, we decided it would be best to say goodbye to Brian and work solely with Norman.

Brian loved show business – he was hooked on the lifestyle and everything that went with it. He owned a Rolls-Royce, and everywhere he went he'd drink champagne. Norman, on the other hand, was a really professional agent, no frills, and was very good at his job. He managed to secure us top rates wherever he could and he also took us into the big time. Whatever you felt about Norman, you couldn't deny that he was good at running his business.

Due to my busy working schedule my married life had run into difficulties. Mavis and I had grown apart, despite the fact that we'd had a second child. She was busy taking care of the children while I was touring, virtually non-stop, with Eddie. Although I wasn't looking for a new relationship, during the Christmas of 1972 an angel walked into my life. Eddie and I were touring in a panto with Diddy David Hamilton at Doncaster, Hanley and Gloucester, appearing for two weeks at each venue. Sheree was one of the dancers and I didn't notice her at first because I was trying to avoid another dancer who fancied me. I have to say that I didn't fancy that other dancer, although I was very flattered by her advances.

One night we all went to a club and I'll always remember noticing Sheree for the first time. She had such big blue eyes. I couldn't take my eyes off her and apparently I asked my brother David (who was our road manager at the time) to ask her for a date on my behalf. She replied that if I wanted to ask her I should do it myself. Well, for me it was love at first sight. I couldn't get her out of my mind. But Sheree was courting at the time and her boyfriend used to come up quite regularly, so I found it difficult to approach her.

Eventually the troupe moved down to Gloucester and I had the opportunity to take Sheree out a few times. When we were together we got on like a house on fire and after the tour I said that I had to see her again. I can still remember going into this pub called The Wheatsheaf in Manchester, across the road from Tweedy's Dance School where Sheree was working out. I used to stay in the pub until Sheree's class had finished and then we'd meet.

Angel eyes

It was February, so it was quite cold, and I'd be looking at the clock, then at the door, then back to the clock again, until she eventually walked through the door. I can see her now in this long brown coat that touched her ankles and a little white knitted cap that covered her long brown hair (which she still has to this day), and those big blue eyes. We'd sit together for ages, just talking. I think the landlord got fed up with us because he wanted to close and we'd still be chatting.

I've discovered that love is a funny thing. It blocks out everything else in your life and all you can think of is the one you love. I simply wanted to be with Sheree all the time. I'd be working in Newcastle and I'd travel all the way home and go straight to her house in Bolton. I'd tap on the window and she would appear and then we'd chat for ages. I just didn't want to go home.

Eventually, the inevitable happened and I had to leave Mavis. I knew it wasn't an easy situation, but I couldn't stand being away from Sheree. People would say, 'Don't be daft, Syd, you're just infatuated.' Well, I'm still infatuated after 26 years and we've been married for 23 of those! People also said it wouldn't last...

My conduct obviously shocked a lot of people, but I think they've realized by now that I made the right decision. I can't understand how people can live with a mistress, leading a double life. It would be impossible for me to do that. I had to be with one or the other. As soon as I knew there was no way back with Sheree, I knew I had to divorce Mavis.

The divorce went through quickly because Mavis knew our relationship was over, but we had two children – Paul and Donna – to consider. Looking back at my first marriage, people might say it was the pressure of my lifestyle that caused us to separate, but this wasn't true. It would have happened even if I'd remained as a painter and decorator. I think, quite simply, that I was too young when I married Mavis. I was very immature then, and perhaps I was under pressure because all my mates were getting married when they were about 21 years old.

In spite of the divorce I was still able to see the children most weekends, but when they approached their teenage years our meetings tended to be less frequent. The first time Sheree saw the children, I had dropped her off in Sale to do a bit of shopping. I then went to their house and collected Paul, who was five, and Donna, who was three. They were sitting in the back of the car waving when we went to pick Sheree up, and I could see her looking at these two little faces. Both children took to her instantly because she was wonderful with them. In later life I had some very difficult meetings with Paul, who was diagnosed as a schizophrenic. When he was being particularly awkward I always felt that Sheree could handle him better than me.

As the years rolled on from 1973 to '76, it got harder to see Paul and Donna because I was so busy performing all over the country. I was in London quite a lot of the time and committed to TV work, so I didn't see them as much as I would have liked. I still feel a certain amount of guilt about that situation, but there was nothing I could do to change it. As a professional entertainer I had to pursue my career wherever it took me.

left With Mum and Peter at Burnage, summer 1943

below The lads on our annual holiday, Isle of Man, 1960

The first publicity shot, in our back garden, summer 1961

At 19, with Eddie (20) at the Oaks Hotel, Manchester, 1961

above and right
Mid-'60s publicity shots

Our first rock and roll tour, with Lulu, 1965

Just married!
With Sheree in
Scarborough,
summer
1975

below Eddie, me, Jim Davidson, Frank Carson, Norman Collier and a friend, Blackpool, summer 1975

left A keep fit campaign for a Liverpool pantomime, 1978

below With Don McLane and George Hamilton at an interview for Don's Sunday morning programme

Meeting Princess Anne at a charity greyhound race, Wembley Stadium, 1985

At Eddie's golf classic
dinner, spring 1994

Filming for *Supersonic
Syd*, Bournemouth 1985

left Painting with Dominic (20 months), Torquay, spring 1990

below With Donna at *This is Your Life*, 1993

Paul, Sheree and Donna, Eastbourne, 1981

My confirmation day, summer 1992

With Dominic and Sheree, 1998

I remember the time when Paul had his accident. He'd been run over by a van and nearly lost his leg. I was stuck down in London in a TV show and couldn't get out to see him. In fact, Sheree took Mavis over to Huddersfield where Paul was having an operation on his leg. They had to break the bone and stretch it (a new operation from Germany) and then the bone was meant to grow again like a stalagmite and stalactite, and eventually the two pieces would bond together. This was undoubtedly a painful operation for Paul, and he was only nine.

Shortly after the accident I was rehearsing for a TV show when a phone call came through from Paul. He was hysterical and quite irate and was telling me that the nurses were hurting him. How he got on the phone I'll never know, because he was supposed to be confined to his bed. Apparently they simply wanted to wash his face, but because he was feeling so irrational he wouldn't let them. Sadly, I couldn't do anything to help because of my work in London. I tried to calm him down and the nurse came on the line and told me that he was hard to handle. That was only one of the many incidents that dogged his life.

In April 1974 Eddie and I were offered the opportunity of appearing at the London Palladium. I knew this was going to be a great experience, but when I found out who was topping the bill it was even better. The star of the show was Cliff Richard. Eddie and I have always admired Cliff – in fact, I think one of the first songs we did together back in the days of the Stonemasons was 'Living Doll', so you can understand our excitement.

We watched Cliff rehearse and we knew we were watching a star. It was unbelievable how he conveyed this inner strength. It was then that I found out he was a Christian. When you meet Christians like Cliff they always seem to have that inner peace. He'd be on stage and everything would be going wrong – mikes would be going off, lights would be in the wrong place – and yet he never got mad. Eddie and I would sit in the stalls watching him and we'd say, 'Come on, Cliff, get mad, get mad,' and he wouldn't. Another thing I discovered was that when you were chatting to him, you'd be the one in a panic and you'd find yourself saying, 'Well, sorry Cliff, I've got to leave now, I'm on stage,' and rushing off, but he was never in a hurry and he'd always take time to listen. I admired him for this and hoped that one day I'd find what he had.

I'll always remember the party he gave on the last night of the show. It was at his flat in the Marylebone Road and Sheree and I were invited. It was a fantastic home. As you walked in you could see all the silver and platinum discs on the wall. I remember that the food was brilliant – it was curry, which I really like, as does Cliff, I think.

If you're ever in Ealing there's a great Indian restaurant there called the Taj Mahal. It was actually one of Cliff's favourite haunts. While we were in London, Sheree and I were always bumping into him there. We met him once after he'd recorded 'A Little in Love'. He came over and said 'hello'.

'Thanks for dedicating the song to me, Cliff,' I said.

'What do you mean?' he asked.

'Well,' I replied, 'a "Little" in Love.' He did laugh.

Anyway, back to the party. The lounge had been cleared of all the furniture and it was like a giant dance floor. Cliff just danced the night away. All the girls from the show were there and I think he had a dance with each one. He must have got through at least six shirts that night because every time we looked at him he was in a different one. If you ever get invited to one of Cliff's parties you're in for a treat, they're brilliant!

Talking about Cliff reminds me of one of the questions I always get asked in show business – 'Who do you admire most?' Well, it's got to be Cliff Richard. I think he's such a generous person because he's heavily involved in charity work, on top of all the performing he does. He's also a great showman and a perfectionist and, let's face it, he's still around after all these years in the business. I really hope he just keeps on performing.

Towards the end of 1974 Sheree and I decided to get married. We wanted the ceremony to be at Sheree's church in Westhoughton, but because I was divorced they refused our request. I was upset for Sheree because she hadn't done anything wrong – she'd just fallen in love with me. We continued to walk up the main street in Westhoughton until we saw this little Methodist church. It looked really run down and it wasn't at all like Sheree's home church. It didn't have any stained-glass windows, and all the railings and the door needed a coat of paint. But that wasn't impor-tant because they welcomed us with open arms. By the day of the wedding the members had arranged for the gate, the railings and the door to be painted. The only trouble was, they'd picked the brightest red you've ever seen!

Our reception was held at a place called Charnock Richard, off the M6. Everyone who attended seemed to have a fabulous time. All our mates and relations were there. At five o'clock in the morning we had to fly from Manchester to Tunisia for our honeymoon – everyone was shattered by then.

When we arrived in Tunisia we went to a place called Hammamet. Sheree and I were both dressed up in smart suits and we walked down to our room, which was a little bungalow in the hotel complex. Opening the door of the bungalow, I put the suitcases down and Sheree flopped onto the bed. I was just about to fall down next to her when she started staring at me. She didn't seem able to speak and she kept pointing at my, well, how can I say it, at my trousers. Naturally I wondered what was wrong with her. She looked really scared. I didn't want to look down (because I'm a bit of a coward) and I thought, 'I wonder if my fly's open?' but she wouldn't have been scared about that. In the end I started to whack whatever was on me with my hand and it turned out to be the biggest grasshopper I'd ever seen. I was so uptight and nervous that I panicked and started to tread all over the poor thing. I was trying desperately to kill it but it wouldn't die, and eventually it hopped off. What a welcome to our honeymoon hotel!

Our wedding and honeymoon were both memorable occasions for Sheree and me. We still keep in touch with that little Methodist church and we even had our son christened there. When it's possible we always try to attend the Christmas Day service. One Christmas my mother-in-law thought the service was at 10.30 a.m., but when we arrived everyone was leaving. Naturally they asked us where we were going and we said, 'We've come for the service.' Well, we soon realized that we'd got the time wrong so we turned round, ready to leave. All of a sudden the leaders called us back. We followed them into the chapel, and do you know what? They did the whole service again just for us. I mean, how many churches would do that for you? I could never repay that congregation for that act of kindness.

Talking about being at home for Christmas makes me think of pantomimes. Eddie and I still perform in pantos and the only day we get off is Christmas Day. But every Christmas we always try to get back home or see Sheree's Mum and Dad if we can. Sometimes it's been more of a struggle than expected.

In 1973, before Sheree and I had got married, we were in Croydon doing the *Leslie Crowther Christmas Cracker*. On Christmas Eve we set off back home, driving in the dark along the M6 with a car full of presents. I was tired and it was foggy. Well, I was trying to pull into Corley Services, which was just being built, and I couldn't actually see the entrance because of the fog. Somehow we ended up wedged on a kerb stone. I'd only had the car about three months and now it was well and truly stuck.

Telling Sheree to sit and wait for me, I got out and stepped into six inches of mud. 'What a great day off!' I thought. I walked up to the services and telephoned a local rescue firm. When the van finally arrived, the men fastened chains to my car and managed to wrench it off the kerb. But they told me I couldn't possibly use the car and it would have to be towed away to their garage.

Meanwhile, Sheree had left the car to find me and she arrived without a scrap of mud on her black suede boots. I couldn't believe she'd managed this. I'm sure she must have walked above the mud (now, where have I heard that story before, or something similar?).

So there we were, sitting slumped at the services with no car. By now it was one o'clock in the morning on Christmas Day. We felt totally depressed and we didn't know what we were going to do. Our only option was to call a taxi. While we were talking this over, a gentleman came up to us and said, 'I just overheard what you were saying. I'm going up to Chester and if you'd like a lift to the Knutsford Services you could get a taxi there and it won't cost you as much.'

We discovered that he was an airline pilot called Philip and we never did know his surname, but we were grateful and thanked him for his offer. Somehow we managed to cram our presents into his car, which was already quite full. He told us that he was going back to his mother's for Christmas. We all piled into his car and set off for Knutsford.

We chatted as we travelled up the motorway, and when we reached our destination, Philip said, 'Where do you live?'

'Westhoughton in Lancashire,' we answered.

'Well,' said Philip, 'I'll take you home.'

We couldn't believe he was prepared to take us all the way to Sheree's parents. Loaded down with our presents, we finally arrived at six in the morning and Philip still had to drive on to his mother's. I wish he'd get in touch with us if he can still remember picking up two bedraggled people on Christmas Day in 1973. The incident made me realize how helpful and kind people can be, and that it's possible for something very positive to happen in a desperate situation. And by the way, I'd still like to know how Sheree avoided that mud!

6

The missing ingredient

During 1976 our producer, Roy Mayoh, was offered the opportunity to make a pilot programme for *The Little and Large Show*. The script was to be written by Tony Hawes, with a lot of help from Roy. One of his brainwaves was to use an unusual band on the show and – would you believe it? – he chose the Ivy Benson All-Girl Band. Ivy Benson, as you'll remember, appeared with us in our first talent competition on the Isle of Man. Eddie and I thought this was a fantastic idea because we didn't think anyone had used a girls' band before.

Our musical director/arranger for the show was a man called Sam Harding and he's a smashing guy, easy going and jolly. The Ivy Benson band are brilliant musicians with their own material, but they really needed quite a bit of a practice with the new numbers for our show. It took them a couple of days to perfect the sound, but in the end it worked a treat.

Thames Television liked the pilot show and in 1977 they gave us our own series. In fact, it replaced the *Opportunity Knocks* slot on a Monday night from 6.45 to 7.30.

While Eddie and I were over the moon with our new contract, we didn't fully realize what we'd let ourselves in for until Roy called us into his office. He sat us down and then produced the biggest pile of scripts we'd ever seen. Placing them on the table, he said, 'Put the first show together, lads,' and left the room.

Eddie and I just looked at each other and our first thought was, 'Let's go home!' but a few moments later Roy appeared and said that he just wanted to scare us a bit. Well, it worked!

In the end, Roy had a change of heart about Ivy Benson, and decided to stick with someone less unusual. He chose a guy called Tony Hatch. Tony is well known as a songwriter and he's written TV themes like *Neighbours*. He also wrote for his wife Jackie Trent, the singer, and she was often in the charts. One song Tony used to do was the Stevie Wonder hit called 'Sir Duke'. Surprisingly, letters poured in from viewers asking how Tony dared to sing such a song. He used to judge a talent show called New Faces and he was always slagging off singers, saying how bad they were. So when he eventually came on our show and was singing not judging, people thought they could get their own back. You can imagine some of the letters he got. Still, it proved to be a great talking point and the controversy gave us some useful publicity.

One of our first guests on that show in 1977 was Matt Munro, who in my opinion was a great guy. I remember

Matt (who was a legend in his own time) walking straight over to Eddie and me, who were very new at the game, and asking what colour suits we'd chosen for the show. We told him we'd got blue ones, and he said he'd chosen the same. To create a contrast we offered to wear a different colour, but he said, 'No, it's your show.' We'd never heard anyone say that to us before. We were so fortunate to have so many well-known faces on that show, including the singing star Demis Roussos.

Television may sound glamorous, but it's hard work and no one worked harder than Roy. We'd start rehearsals at ten o'clock in the morning and work through until ten at night. We recorded the show on the Saturday and it went out on the following Monday.

As you might expect, the first show was very nerve-racking. Our agents at the time were Norman Murray and Anne Chudley and they were sitting in the audience. Norman, as I've said before, wasn't the most tactful man and he could be downright rude. After the first show Eddie and I were on cloud nine and we were congratulating ourselves, thinking we'd done the best show in the world. Yes, there'd been a few disasters, but we'd spotted them and all we wanted now was to get to the bar and have a few drinks. But when we finally arrived at the bar, Norman was waiting. He laid into us and said that it was the most amateur show he'd ever seen. Now you may or may not believe this, but I saw Eddie break down and cry because Norman was attacking us so ferociously.

Fortunately, at this point Roy walked in and recognizing what Norman had done, he pulled him to one side. He then proceeded to tell him what he thought of his conduct and banned him from coming to the rest of the shows. After that incident things ran smoothly until the last show, which was cancelled because of a strike by the ITV electricians. Despite this hitch, we still managed to climb to number 13 in the ratings.

As you might appreciate, Roy was over the moon about the success of the series. He'd really stuck his neck out to get us the contract and now it had paid off for everybody. The only disappointment we experienced was connected with a group called The Nobodies. This was the group who'd tried to help my Dad the night he died. Well, we decided to get them on our show because they were a good act, so they turned up, but that was the show which was cancelled at the last minute.

With nothing to do, Eddie and I returned to our hotel, the Cardinal Wolsey, and we decided to arrange an impromptu get-together with the cast. We were all fed up, especially The Nobodies, because this should have been one of their big breaks. In those days appearing on TV was a big bonus and we were hoping this would launch them into stardom. Anyway, our plan hadn't come off, and they were really sick. So, to drown our sorrows, we all went to the bar. The group set up all their gear in the corner of the room and we had a jam session which, if I remember correctly, went on until the early hours of the morning.

As our fame grew Eddie and I were exposed to the dealings of what some people call 'the gutter press'. A reporter from a well-known Sunday paper came to interview us because we were appearing in our first show. Having invited us for a meal, we soon discovered that all he wanted to do was to try to nail us for something. He kept emphasizing the fact that I was divorced and had left my children to run off with a young dancer.

During our meeting two young girls came into the restaurant and asked Eddie and me for our autographs, so we said, 'Yes, certainly.' Once we'd signed our names the girls disappeared. But almost immediately this reporter asked us if they were waiting for us back at the hotel. We couldn't believe what this guy was insinuating. He was actually trying to suggest that these young girls were with us, when in fact we'd never met them before. He came back to the hotel with us, saying that we could have a drink together, but I'm sure he was looking for the girls. We couldn't convince him they were just autograph hunters. When the article was published, to our relief it really wasn't too bad. We found out later that the editor's daughter was a big fan and so he'd decided not to use anything sleazy. Mind you, I believe there were a few rewrites before it was published!

The years that followed our TV success seemed to fly by. I found it very difficult to get the time to see my children, Paul and Donna, and Sheree and I were only together at weekends. Naturally this put a strain on Sheree because I hardly ever saw her. I was stuck down in London while she was looking after our house in the north. She'd visit me whenever she could and she called to see Paul now and again.

The missing ingredient

It was a time in our lives when the world and his wife wanted us. Even though we'd only completed one series with Thames, our place in the ratings meant we had celebrity status. Despite the success of our show, Thames were still deliberating about another series when Michael Hurll from the BBC stepped in. We were performing in a seaside special in Great Yarmouth at the time, and we tore the place apart (they were really great shows)!

Michael came backstage to see us and said, 'I suppose you're doing another series for Thames?'

'We don't know,' we replied.

'Is it okay to approach your manager?'

'Well, yes,' we told him. The next thing we knew, we had a three-year contract with the BBC, which eventually lasted 14 years!

In 1977 we were booked to do a summer season at Blackpool at the North Pier and Norman told us we were the top of the bill. 'Who else is on the bill with us?' we asked him.

'Norman Collier, Frank Carson and a young comedian called Jim Davidson,' he told us.

Eddie and I were very flattered to be supported by so much talent, but we said, 'No way, we can't top that lot.'

But Norman just said, 'Yes you can.' And to be honest, at that time of our careers, we could! On the first night Jim started the show and stormed them, then Norman went on and paralysed them, and then Frank Carson went on. During the interval our producer saw two old ladies get up and leave the hall, so he chased after them.

'Excuse me ladies,' he called, 'the show's not over yet. This is just the interval. You've still got to see Little and Large.'

'Oh we know,' they told him, 'but we can't laugh any more or we'll wet our knickers!'

One night Eddie came in and said he didn't feel well. He was complaining of a tummy pain. The company manager contacted the theatre doctor and when he walked in he was dressed like James Bond. He had the black shirt, white coat, gold rings and several chains round his neck. After he'd taken Eddie's temperature he discovered it was well above normal, so he pulled a couple of packets out of his pocket and handed them to me, saying that I was to give them to Eddie and he'd be back later.

How Eddie got through that next performance I'll never know. Perhaps it was the thought of a game of golf the next day! He was obviously hoping it was nothing serious and was just an attack of indigestion. After the show Eddie went backstage and when he sat down he looked terrible. When the doctor returned he took hold of Eddie and walked him to the end of the pier to ensure that he got into his car and drove home OK.

That week Sheree and I were staying on a boat we'd rented at Garstang, which is about 10 miles away from Blackpool. There were no telephones or any other means of communication on the canal boat so I was quite cut off. The following night when I arrived back in Blackpool, I was walking down towards the promenade when I saw this big sign which said, 'Due to illness, the act of Little and Large will not be appearing tonight.'

The missing ingredient

I couldn't believe it. No one had informed me! While I was rushing along the pier I met Frank Carson. He told me that he'd been trying to reach me, but because I hadn't got a phone it had been impossible. He went on to say that Eddie had been taken to hospital with peritonitis – another 24 hours and he'd have been dead.

Due to Eddie's illness we were laid off for six weeks. To be honest, I think it should have been a lot longer, but Eddie was fed up because Frank Carson kept telling him how good he was at topping the bill! Don't get me wrong, Frank is still our big buddy to this day, but he can't half talk!

Question: What's the difference between Frank Carson and the M1?
Answer: You can turn off the M1!

Talking of Frank reminds me of a funny incident that happened around Eddie's birthday that year. We'd all planned to throw a party for Eddie, but because he was taken ill it had to be cancelled. Frank had already bought the cake, so in order not to waste it he put an advert in the local paper: 'Birthday cake for sale – would suit someone with the name Eddie, aged 36.' He did manage to sell it to an Eddie but he was 42!

With time on my hands while Eddie was recuperating, Sheree and I decided to take Paul and Donna and Sheree's young brother Tracy on a canal trip, and it turned out to be one of the better weeks we had with Paul. We hired a 42-foot long-boat with six berths, a shower and all the necessary mod. cons, and we set out from a place in the Midlands called Stone.

The trip was going well until we reached the first lock. The owners had given us a rough idea of how to pass through one, but when it came to putting theory into practice things weren't quite so easy. We manoeuvred the boat into the lock and closed the doors, and I told Paul and Tracy that when we got to the top they should jump off and tie the boat up. As the water level rose they dutifully jumped off and then immediately jumped back on board again.

'What's the matter with you two?' I said.

'There's a dog on the footpath!' they replied.

Well, I lost my rag and with Sheree holding the wheel, I jumped off the deck shouting, 'What's the matter, are you frightened of a little dog?'

I turned round and came face to face with the biggest Irish Wolfhound I'd ever seen. I was back on the boat in seconds. Luckily the dog was quite friendly and so was the lock keeper, who came out of his cottage to help us after hearing all the commotion.

I'd never been on a long-boat before, but it was an enjoyable experience. It was a lovely time of year because all the trees were covered in blossom. It was very relaxing to be on the water in the middle of the countryside, and at night we would secure the boat and enjoy a meal as we watched the sun go down.

Here are a couple of hints for you, though, after my boating experiences. Firstly, don't sit down for dinner when you're in a lock. I remember one occasion when Sheree had just showered Donna and sat her down in her nightie to eat a stew. I was at the helm and the lads were holding the rope. As we came up to the top of the lock the two boys pulled, the boat banged into the side, and Donna's stew slipped off the table into her lap, poor child. Sheree came up on deck and gave us a mouthful, and it certainly wasn't stew! Secondly, try not to cover too much ground in one trip. We did 90 miles in a week and I think a third of that would have been enough.

When Eddie had recovered we finished the season in Blackpool, and shortly afterwards we were invited to appear on the *Royal Variety Show*. Everything was happening so fast that we couldn't believe our good fortune. At the beginning of 1977 we were performing in our own TV series, then we went on to a record-breaking summer season and now we were to appear on the *Variety Show*. All in just one year!

This particular year was designed to celebrate the Queen's Jubilee. Because of this special occasion the Americans had bought the rights to the show and wanted it to be called 'America's Tribute to Her Majesty the Queen'. As a result of the American influence nearly all the artists were international stars. There was Bob Hope, Julie Andrews, Shirley Maclaine, Rudolph Nureyev, Rich Little – the list went on and on. In fact, I think there were only three acts from Britain: Tommy Cooper, Brotherhood of Man and Little and Large.

During one of the rehearsals Bob Hope was going through his lines and instead of remembering them, he was using a man who held up boards. But when it came to our introduction he called us 'Little and George'. Eddie and I looked at each other and said, 'Who's going to tell Bob he's got it wrong?' Luckily one of the producers stepped in and suggested that the cards were enlarged so that Bob could see the words more clearly.

Eddie and I sat in the theatre and watched all these legends from the entertainment world rehearsing. It really took our breath away. We said to each other, 'What are we doing here?'

During one rehearsal two gentlemen came over and introduced themselves. One was Lord Bernard Delfont and the other was Lew Grade.

Lord Delfont said to Lew Grade, 'This is Syd and Eddie, Little and Large, Lew.'

Lew said, 'Hello boys, how long are you down for, three minutes?'

'No, it's nine, actually,' we told him.

'Nine minutes! No, it can't be. Nobody does nine minutes.'

We got the impression that he assumed only the top stars would be doing nine minutes, not newcomers like us. But that brief conversation gave us a chance to meet two very influential men and we felt honoured that they should take the time to introduce themselves. I have to say, having met them, that they were beautifully portrayed on *Spitting Image*!

Once the show had started, we appeared in our nine-minute spot and I think it went down well. To be honest, I can't really remember because it went so fast. Still, we got a good cheer at the end.

It was part of the tradition of the *Royal Variety Show* that all the stars lined up afterwards to meet the Queen, Prince Charles and the Duke of Edinburgh. As I was standing in the line, the royal party walked along and started asking questions of the performers, such as 'What have you been doing?'

Shirley Maclaine said, 'I've just finished a film in Hollywood.'

Next were the Muppets, and Prince Charles asked, 'What are you doing at the moment?' and they said, 'We're doing a movie in the Caribbean.'

Bob Hope mentioned that he was off to some other exotic location.

Then it came to us and the Queen said, 'Where are you appearing?' and we had to tell her, 'Stoke-on-Trent ma'am'. They probably had a bit of a laugh about us, but it was the truth, because as soon as we'd finished the *Variety Show* we were back at Jollies in Stoke.

Out of all the famous stars who appeared on that show, the man who stole it for me was Tommy Cooper. He was such an unbelievably funny man. There are lots of comedians around today but there aren't many funny men. Tommy was simply one of the best. Eddie and I and Rich Little were sitting in the make-up department backstage and we were watching Tommy's spot on the screen. Tommy was scheduled to appear for 14 minutes and in that time he tore the place apart. It was an all-British audience so you can imagine that they really appreciated him. But when Eddie and I looked at Rich Little we realized that he simply couldn't grasp the point of his act.

The Amercians have a dry sense of humour that's very verbal, whereas Tommy's routines were visual. He'd be doing all these silly jokes like tossing flowers over his shoulder as if the Queen had thrown them out of the Royal Box, then he'd say 'For me?' He'd then appear with a giant sword, which he dropped on the floor, kneeling on one knee as if the Queen was going to knight him. It was pure Tommy and very funny, but Rich Little couldn't see this. Instead, he kept saying, 'What's he doing now?' or 'What does that mean?' It was strange because to Eddie and me it was all so obvious.

As I said, Tommy was down for 14 minutes but he actually finished after 28. Understandably, the directors were pulling their hair out and saying things like, 'When's this man coming off?' But you couldn't stop Tommy when he was in full flow and that night he was fantastic.

The *Variety Show* always reminds me of a gentleman called George Childs, who was a self-made millionaire. We'd met him up in the north-east of England and he had a genuine love of show business. Our friendship started in a club called Le Strada in Sunderland and whenever we were booked to appear there he'd come and see us. Over the years he became a great friend, until his death a few years ago.

On one occasion George gave me a ukulele. It must be well over 50 years old now, because he said he bought it when he was courting his wife Dorothy. Even though I've spent a lot of my career playing the guitar, I still enjoy the ukulele and I'll play it when the mood takes me. Mind you, I'm not as good as George was. He was a mean player. I'm very proud of that gift and I suppose you could say that I treasure it like an heirloom.

George and Dorothy had made Eddie and me a promise back in the '60s. 'When you're on the *Royal Variety Show*,' they said, 'we'll be in the front row.' Well, believe it or not, in 1977 they were both in the audience. They weren't in the front row but they were there all the same, just as they'd promised. It was wonderful to know that they were there, and I think it had a calming effect on us. When you're on stage and doing something exciting you can lose your nerve, but seeing George with his big smile was very reassuring. After the show we all celebrated with dinner at the Savoy.

On the night of the show Sheree was also in the audience, along with lots of our friends. I'll never forget how beautiful she looked. She couldn't find a dress that she liked so her Mum made her one. It was a copy of a dress worn by Barbra Streisand – full-length and black, with a plunging neckline and diamante decoration. She had a little skull cap to match and she looked gorgeous. Sheree's Mum was good at making dresses, and could put something together in a flash. Sheree would say to her, 'Syd's coming round and he's taking me out. I've got nothing to wear,' and in no time at all she'd made her an outfit.

For the next few years everything ran smoothly with my career. The wave of success that Eddie and I were on just didn't stop. However, in my personal life there was a disappointment. In 1983 Sheree and I celebrated nine years of marriage and the only thing that was missing was a baby. I think that Eddie's wife, Patsy, had given birth to Ryan that year and it affected Sheree, because we avoided taking precautions and she still wasn't pregnant. Eventually Sheree went for tests and that's when we decided to see Mr Steptoe at a fertility clinic called Bourne Hall.

Bourne Hall is a mansion stuck in the middle of the countryside, and as you approach it you can feel as if you're stepping back in time. It's not hard to visualize horse-drawn coaches coming up to the main entrance and a team of butlers and maids gathered round the front door waiting to greet you.

As you step into the entrance hall you can see that little has changed over the years. There's a wooden staircase, which reminded me of the scene from *Gone with the Wind* when Scarlett O'Hara stands on the stairs and Brett Butler goes out of the door and utters those immortal words, 'Frankly, my dear, I don't give a damn!' However, as you walk away from the hall towards the back of the house you are brought smack up to date with the latest technology. Things might have changed since our visit, but in the '80s a lot of the work seemed to take place in Portakabins that surrounded the property.

The staff at the hall made us feel very welcome, although Sheree and I were very nervous. Leaving Sheree there by herself was one of the hardest things I've ever had to do and my journey back to London seemed to last forever.

The missing ingredient

While Sheree was detained at the clinic, Eddie and I were in the middle of a TV series. I decided not to tell anyone that Sheree and I were trying for a test-tube baby, and that included Eddie. My reason was to avoid any disappointment if the whole procedure didn't work, and then no one would be any the wiser.

Away from the studios I was staying in a pub called Ye Olde White Bear in Hampstead Heath. The landlady and landlord, Stan and Julie, were two old friends of ours. Julie was a great friend of Sheree's from her dancing days because they'd appeared together in a summer show in Scarborough. Over the years they'd stayed in touch, even when Julie had married Stan and given birth to Charlie, our godchild. Stan died in Bangkok in 1995, but we've remained close friends with Julie and Charlie.

About a week after Sheree had arrived at Bourne Hall I was starting to get panicky. The doctor had told us that at a certain time of the month Sheree's eggs would be fertile and I would be needed to provide a sperm sample. Because I was worried that I'd be called away in the middle of our TV show, I decided to tell Eddie and Bill Wilson (our producer) about the clinic after all. Incidentally, I think Bill was the man who kept us on the 'box'. He knew everything about comedy and had a great ability as a director. He was the man who made me study my act more carefully. I accept that I'm not a natural performer, so nothing was ever easy for me, but Bill would come on the floor and teach me how to see things in a different way. He helped me a lot and it was a pleasure working with him. In fact, it was a double pleasure because his lovely wife Kath makes a mean curry!

Once I'd told Bill and Eddie about my personal life I could tell they were relieved, especially Eddie. We'd worked together so long that we'd got to know each other very well and in that situation it's hard to conceal things. And because Sheree wasn't around, Eddie thought we'd split up. When I told him what we were up to he was over the moon.

The long-awaited call from Bourne Hall came on one of our rehearsal days, so this meant I could rush up to Cambridge to do my bit and then get back to work. I don't think I want to go into details, and all I'll say is that first of all they stick a test tube in your hand, then you're put in a room with a pile of magazines and told that these might be helpful if you're having difficulty. Well, I did as I was told, but never again. It was so embarrassing!

After 10 days I returned to collect Sheree. It was Guy Fawkes night and I can remember motoring along the driveway at Bourne Hall and seeing this big bonfire blazing away. We said our goodbyes to the medical staff and they told us that it was up to nature now and they'd let us know if the method had worked.

On our way home Sheree said that she didn't want to go back to Bourne Hall even if things didn't work out, but she told me how nice everybody had been and about the people she'd met. All of them were childless and they'd been trying for years to have a baby. One lady was determined to keep attending Bourne Hall until she conceived, so I really hope things worked out for her. While Sheree was there she met women from all walks of life, including ordinary working ladies and foreign princesses.

Two weeks later we were in the White Bear with Julie and Stan when Sheree announced that she had to phone Bourne Hall. She'd apparently started her menstrual cycle and this wasn't a good sign. Sensing that this was an intimate moment, Stan and Julie tried to make themselves invisible by not making a sound. Bless them! I can still picture them holding one another in a corner as far away from us as possible.

Sheree picked up the phone and asked to speak to her doctor, and she then told him what had happened. He said to her that he was very sorry but the treatment obviously hadn't worked. I think he phrased it a bit better than that, but I wasn't on the phone so I didn't hear his exact words.

Replacing the receiver, Sheree said something totally unexpected to me. 'It's just you and me now kid', were her words. I didn't know what to make of this reaction to such disappointing news at the time, but looking back I think she was telling me she'd had enough. She didn't want to try this method again, instead she felt that we had to get on with our lives. Feeling deeply emotional, we just held each other tightly for what seemed like ages until the phone rang. It turned out to be the doctor again. He was concerned because Sheree had sounded so calm. He simply wanted to know if she was okay.

Having made this decision over Bourne Hall, we did get on with our lives, but it was hard for Sheree in the years that followed. We'd go to show-biz parties and charity dos where people would start talking to us, and nine times out of ten the question would come up, 'Have you got any children?' or 'When are you going to start a family?' or 'You've been married that long – no children?' You can't blame people because they didn't know our predicament, but I knew how much these questions hurt Sheree, and I couldn't say much because I had Paul and Donna from my first marriage.

Being childless is a bit like getting a new car, say a Ford Escort. Before you bought one, you never took too much notice of them, but as soon as you buy one you see hundreds. Well, it was a bit like that for us regarding children. In the past we hadn't thought much about children, but when we wanted one, everybody else seemed to have one and wherever you went people would be talking about them. So many conversations were centred around children and what they were doing. Ladies always seemed to be saying things like 'my lad was walking when he was 11 months', or 'my baby sleeps for 10 hours'.

Excluded from this line of chatter, I used to look at Sheree and see that she was hurt. I just felt like screaming at the top of my voice, 'Shut up about your children!' But these people were innocent, they didn't know what we were going through and it certainly wasn't their fault. They were, after all, simply showing how proud they were of their offspring – and would you believe we've been saying exactly the same sort of things about Dominic? Oops! Now I've gone and let the cat out of the bag!

7

Our little miracle

My work in the '80s fell into a routine of a Christmas panto, then a summer season followed by our TV series. In 1985 after a hard summer season Sheree and I took a week's holiday, and it turned out that a week of sun and fun proved to be just the tonic we needed.

Feeling refreshed, we flew back to Manchester airport looking forward to meeting Sheree's parents, who'd offered to collect us. When we saw them, though, we knew something was wrong. They were holding hands and looking very solemn. Naturally, all sorts of things shot through my mind. Had we been burgled? Had Paul been playing up again? But none of my suspicions was correct. They said that my Mum had suffered a heart attack. The shock of the news caused Sheree to grab hold of me and start to cry. Her parents went on to say that my Mum was still at home but really wasn't well.

We all piled into the car and drove straight to my Mum's, where Linda and my brother's wife Sonia were waiting for us. When I saw Mum she seemed so frail. I bent down to give her a kiss and a cuddle, but I instinctively knew she was seriously ill.

In that moment I thought back to the time when I'd first introduced Sheree to her. You can imagine what her first impression might have been and she probably thought of her as the scarlet woman! But I was so pleased with Mum because she soon got to like her. When we left after that first meeting, Sheree leaned forward and kissed Mum on the cheek. I could tell she was a bit surprised. Even her own children never kissed her, especially us lads because we thought that was soppy – but then Sheree's family are all affectionate. Sheree said afterwards that maybe she shouldn't have kissed Mum.

'Did I do the wrong thing?' she asked me.

'No, I don't think so, why?'

'She seemed surprised!'

Anyway, the second time we went round, Sheree didn't offer a kiss and my Mum turned to her and said, 'Where's my kiss?' So after that request, we always kissed her at the end of every visit.

Sheree's affectionate nature made me realize that as people we can be scared of showing love. I really believe that if people were more open with their feelings the world would be a better place. But at least in our relationship the ritual was established and it was lovely to think that Mum had the opportunity to show affection for once. Don't get me wrong

– Mum loved her kids, but she came from a big family of 13 and I don't think Grandma and Granddad had much time for kissing!

Going back to Mum's present predicament, though, our Linda told me that Mum had suffered the heart attack in the middle of the night. She'd fallen out of bed and couldn't move. It was Auntie Jessie who raised the alarm the next day when Mum hadn't turned up for the meeting she'd arranged with her. Wanting to know why she was so delayed, Auntie Jessie called in at the house and found her. Now, standing at her bedside looking at her suddenly frail face, I remembered a comment she'd once made to me: 'I know what people mean when they say they're dead tired.'

The doctors told us that it was only a matter of time before Mum died because her heart had been damaged too badly. She was transferred to Wythenshawe Hospital, and Sheree and I would go to see her there, sitting on her bed to chat to her. She would always put her head on Sheree's coat because it had a big fur collar and she said it was the softest thing she'd ever rested on. We could tell that Mum wasn't well because she'd stay in that position for ages. Later, when Sheree got rid of that coat, she removed the collar as a keepsake.

One night the hospital phoned and asked if we'd come straight over. When we arrived we found that Mum had passed away. Nothing in life can prepare you for losing a loved one, especially when it's a parent.

My Mum and Dad were from the 'old school' and they believed that you only went to the doctor if you were dying.

I'm sure Dad must have had warnings about his heart. I remember Mum saying once, when he came home from work, that he thought he was a goner. He'd apparently run for the bus and when he climbed on board he found he couldn't get his breath back. Mum told me that this had happened to Dad on several occasions, yet she was just the same and would shrug off any warning signs. She'd complain about indigestion pains or not being able to walk, but she wouldn't go to the doctor's. She got told off by the doctor once for smoking and I think that's why she wouldn't go back.

When each of my parents died it was sudden, especially with Dad because he was only 50 years old. With Mum I thought, 'No, she was never ill,' and with Dad, 'He was too young.' Then you ask yourself, 'Why Mum, why Dad?' I take comfort in the thought that they both had a fairly good time on this earth, but I bet they're having a better time up there!

Writing about my parents brings to mind my Uncle George, who I told you about briefly in an earlier chapter. Sadly, he passed away while I was writing this book. This seems an appropriate place to tell you about him because he was very close to my parents.

George wasn't really my uncle – he was my Dad's best mate. He'd known him since he was a teenager and so I'd known him and Auntie Peggy all my life. George had one of those infectious laughs that made everybody else join in, and in the early years he liked a drink. He also loved children and we always had some fun when Uncle George was about. One winter's day, Peter, David, Linda and I were making a snowman and we were having a great time when, all of a sudden, we were pelted with snowballs. It was Uncle George and my Dad and they'd come home from a lunch-time session at the pub where they'd obviously had a few pints. They must have been around the corner of the house making snowballs for some time, because the fight went on for ages. Mind you, we got our own back and they finished up wetter than us.

When my Dad was in the RAF, Uncle George used to look after Mum because she was pregnant with me. He was a steeplejack and he stayed around until he had to go down south to Devon and knock down landmarks such as tall chimneys. Apparently it was vital that these buildings were removed because the Germans would use them as markers for their bombing raids. It was in Devon that George met his wife Peggy. My Mum was always going down there to visit them both, especially towards the end of her life.

Thinking about these two and my Mum and Dad reminds me of a sequence in a film. I don't know if you've seen the *Star Wars* films, but in *Return of the Jedi* there's a scene at the end when Luke Skywalker's Dad (Darth Vader), Obi-wan Kenobi and Yoda all appear in a sepia-toned image, standing on a hill in another world, smiling back at Luke. Somehow that sequence always makes me think of my family and Uncle George. I like to think of them smiling down at me. I know it may sound daft, but it's something I find very comforting.

The mid-'80s proved to be a time of arrivals and departures. My brother David wanted to stop being our roadie at this time. He lived in Poole and it was so far away from Eddie and myself. There was really too much travelling involved and he was a family man, so he decided to call it a day. When he left we replaced him with a guy called Derek Wyborne, who's still our road manager today.

I'm not decrying David in any way, but when we hired him he hadn't had any experience so he didn't really know what to do, and we didn't know what to expect. But when Derek arrived he sort of took over. He carried our suits and looked after my guitar, and everything was set up on stage before we knew it. And we didn't have this thing going where I had to explain our relationship to everyone. Because Derek wasn't my brother it seemed that things worked out better. However, Eddie and I quickly discovered that Derek enjoys driving and loves vehicles – and this can be expensive. He's always getting new tyres and things for the van, but I suppose that's part of his job and he's very good at it!

It was during the mid-'80s that Eddie and I decided we weren't happy with Norman Murray, our agent. We were finding it difficult because he was quite a hard person and people used to say, 'We don't like dealing with Norman,' so we decided it was time to part company. The parting was quite amicable, but we didn't have anybody in mind to replace him. All we knew was that we didn't want to be with Norman any longer. While we were on the lookout for a replacement manager Eddie had a chat with his great friend Jimmy Tarbuck. Jimmy said that his agent was very reliable and good at his job, so he suggested we contact Peter Prichard. When we approached Peter and asked him if he'd like to manage us, he said he'd be proud and privileged to do so. Peter and his wife Joan are lovely people, and everybody we spoke to had nothing but the highest respect for Peter. It seemed everybody liked him. This was obviously the right move in our career, because he still looks after us today!

I can still remember the first time Eddie and I went out with Peter and Joan. They invited us to an Italian restaurant in the West End of London. Peter said that we were going to this particular restaurant because they accepted dogs. We thought this was all a bit strange, but he mentioned something about his own dog called Major. Eddie and I arrived at the restaurant and saw Peter and Joan, so we made our way to their table. We were looking around for the dog, and because it was called Major we naturally assumed it was an Alsatian or Rottweiler.

As we sat down we asked, 'Have you brought your dog, Peter?'

'Yes,' he said, 'it's under the table.'

Well, we looked down rather nervously, and there was this little Chihuahua looking like a drowned rat. And we'd been expecting some huge monster... Sadly Major is no longer with us, which is a shame because Peter and Joan were very attached to him.

Back on the home front, Sheree and I were living in Preston at this time. We'd bought a big house, but we found it was quite a drain on our finances. Everything we earned seemed to go on the house. I'd just finished doing a summer season in Torquay and I was very taken with the place and felt tempted to move. Sheree's Mum and Dad lived with us, so any decision we made about moving naturally affected them. We held a family meeting and Sheree and I said we'd like to move to Torquay and they were perfectly welcome to come with us or stay in Preston. Before we had time to finish speaking they'd agreed to come with us.

Our decision was made during the property boom of 1987 and we were offered some terrible houses. It's no wonder estate agents get such a bad name. Some of the house descriptions were unbelievable. One that really made us laugh was a reference to 'sea peeps'. The property sheet said something like 'Lovely views and sea peeps'. Well, we wondered what this meant until we went to see the house for ourselves. For a start it was nowhere near the sea.

After we'd looked round we said to the owner, 'What does this "sea peeps" mean?'

'Well,' she replied, 'if you pop your head out of this window and look round the corner you can just see the sea.'

We couldn't stop laughing. But I have to say, that type of description cropped up a lot in Torquay. The town is built on a hill and some of the gardens were so steep that an Everest climber wouldn't have attempted them! One property we went to see was beautiful – a dream cottage with a thatched roof, genuine old beams and open fires. However, when we arrived we discovered that the photographer had deliberately avoided showing the adjoining pig farm. I'm sure you can imagine what the place smelt like. I didn't have a bacon butty for ages after that!

Our little miracle

After five visits down to Torquay staying with Auntie Peggy and Uncle George we chose a place. Everywhere we go we like to refurbish our home, but this property was a challenge: everything needed to be changed and it was a lot of work. Fortunately, we were all in favour of a new look, and because I've got the best in-laws in the world, Dad – bless him – was a big help. (From our very first meeting I've always called Sheree's parents Mum and Dad.) So they coped with us while we were surrounded by boxes and chaos for the first six months and I can show you a video to prove it. I remember that when we first moved down with all our belongings, we took Auntie Cissy with us because she wasn't very well and Sheree had offered to nurse her. Well, we were so buried by boxes that on one occasion we actually lost her behind them!

It was due to our move to Torquay that I was introduced to a wonderful group of Christian people at the local church. I've always loathed the term 'born-again Christian' because I prefer the term 'rediscovered'. I'm sure there are a lot of people out there who've been through the same format as me: Mum and Dad had me christened, then off to Sunday School (I quite liked that!), joining the Cubs, then the Scouts, followed by a stint with the church choir. Then it was a case of going to church for a while but finding it too boring, so you looked elsewhere in your teenage years for something more interesting. However, in my early life I do remember that I was affected by my Auntie Ethel. She became a devout Catholic and in her sitting room I can recall seeing that famous picture of Jesus holding a lamp and knocking on a door. I used to stare intently at that picture and I think it touched me somehow.

As I grew up, the only time we went to church was for weddings, funerals and christenings. All through my twenties and thirties I was too busy working on my career to think about my spiritual life. I felt that I didn't need God because I was doing quite well without Him, so I only made the occasional visit to the little Methodist church in Westhoughton where Sheree and I had been married. When we moved down to Torquay, however, Sheree's Mum became involved with the Mothers' Union at a church called St Matthias. One day she suggested to Sheree and me that we go to church. At first I thought, 'Oh no, I don't want to do that,' but we did go, and I think that was the time I rediscovered God.

St Matthias is a lovely church, so if you're ever in Torquay do pop in and see Peter Larkin, the vicar, and his wife Molly – they'll both make you feel very welcome. Peter has done a lot for the Third-World countries and I've always thought that if he'd been around a century ago he'd have been a missionary. Two other members of the congregation we particularly got to know were Janice and Priscilla, who've since been ordained. There are so many friendly people in that congregation that I can't mention them all or this book would be too long!

The church held lovely services, which sadly a lot of the older people didn't like (in fact I think some actually left the church to find a quieter one). But Peter liked the idea of attracting young people and it paid off. He wasn't scared of using youngsters with their guitars and other instruments in a Sunday service, and he liked to stage plays, which was good because it kept the children occupied!

On the first Saturday of every month the men would have a breakfast at the church. Afterwards they'd sit down for an hour to talk about anything they wanted to, and at the end they'd pray. The first time I went I showed myself up. When the meal was finished they had a collection and everybody contributed 50p. I thought it would help if I gave a fiver, but one of the lads, called Douglas, said, 'Take it back, Syd, it's only to cover the breakfast,' so after that I gave 50p like everyone else!

These breakfasts were the first meetings I'd been to where you were able to talk to God away from the more formal setting of a church. Actually it felt good, because it was on a more intimate basis and everyone was invited to pray for someone else, never themselves. It's never easy to talk about intimate problems in front of people you don't know, but that barrier seems to lift when you involve God.

This was a lovely time in my life and I was able to get to church most Sundays. Sheree and I had been attending St Matthias for a while when she suggested that we should do something to help. As you know, churches always need money, whether it's for a leaky roof or repairs to the heating system.

'How about a coffee morning?' said Sheree's Mum.

'They all do that,' Sheree replied.

So I added, jokingly, 'What about a karaoke night?'

They both thought this was a great idea so we asked Peter if we could have the hall for a fund-raising event and he agreed. He asked what we were going to do, and we told him about our idea. 'Oh, very nice,' he said, and walked away. The next day we saw Peter in the village and he told me that he'd chatted to most of the elders and told them about our plan, but they wanted to know what a karaoke was. I couldn't believe it. They didn't know what a karaoke was? They do now!

Before the day arrived, Mum and Sheree arranged all the food and wine and I organized the karaoke. The whole evening was hilarious, with Peter, our vicar, singing 'A Hard Day's Night', the church warden singing 'Sixteen Tons', and most of the older congregation singing songs that you'd never even have expected them to know! I'd assumed they could only recite hymns...

As always there was a raffle and I couldn't believe the response I got from some of the friends I'd performed with in pantomimes and summer seasons. When I asked for donations, people like Frank Bruno gave us a pair of autographed boxing gloves and Cliff Richard sent a signed album. They were just two of the many people who were kind enough to find the time to help us. Celebrities must get asked for donations all the time, but the fact that they did it for me was brilliant. In fact, when you go to a major charity 'do' you very rarely see things like that. Can you imagine how much Frank Bruno's gloves would fetch? Not surprisingly, we raised over £700 that night with our little 'do', and naturally everybody wanted to do it again.

Not long after our church karaoke I had to leave the comforts of home and Torquay and return to London, where Eddie and I were contracted to work for about four months. To be honest, I'm not a lover of London. To my mind it always was, and still is, an unfriendly place. We always used to say that even if you walked down the street with no clothes on, no one would take any notice.

While I was busy working, Sheree realized that she'd put on a lot of weight. And, because her fingers had swollen, she was worried that her wedding ring might have to be cut off. Well, that problem was solved, because in the next six months she shed six stone. By the middle of 1987 she was very thin and I was getting worried because she'd previously been diagnosed as anorexic when she was at boarding school.

Most of Sheree's young life had been involved with dancing – she'd started at the age of three. When she went to boarding school her ambition was to be a ballerina, which wasn't a problem until she became a teenager. Although she gained all the degrees she needed and was a fantastic ballerina, her body wasn't the required shape. Teachers can tell if the student ballerinas are going to be big boned, and as you know they really need to be skinny and petite. The teachers realized that Sheree was going to be too big and that was the problem. The news upset Sheree very much and she went on a diet. I think that's when she became anorexic.

Now, all these years later, it seemed that the condition had returned: she was only eating an apple a day. And although I wanted to help her, there was only one person who could change the situation and that was Sheree herself. Her dieting took her down to seven and a half stone and you could see that she wasn't going to stop there.

I'd just finished in London and was due to appear in a pantomime in Liverpool, where Sheree and I were staying in a hotel. We were recovering from the opening night party which had involved plenty of drinking and eating, when Sheree complained of feeling unwell. She said she'd got an upset tummy. 'It must have been a bad pork pie,' she told me. But her condition didn't improve and she kept being sick, so we went to the doctor.

He asked all the usual questions and finished with a lot of womanly things. Then he said, 'Sheree, I think you're pregnant.'

'I can't be!' she replied. 'We can't have children!'

We told him all about Bourne Hall, but he still insisted that she was pregnant. Handing her a pregnancy test kit, he told her to get up at six o'clock the next morning and use it. If the stick turned pink she was pregnant. Well, we both woke up at six and I don't think either of us had slept. Bleary-eyed, we went into the bathroom. Sheree followed the doctor's instructions and then showed me the stick. It turned out to be the brightest pink you've ever seen. We just looked at each other and said, 'It can't be true!'

A week later we had an appointment at the Liverpool General Hospital where Sheree was booked in for a scan. As we waited our turn, there were three other couples also in the queue. Sheree and I felt like grandma and granddad – one of the girls was wearing a gymslip with little white socks and a ponytail; she couldn't have been more than 15 years old. Our turn came, so Sheree went in, and the nurse turned on the machine and took pictures of Sheree's tummy.

'Now there's the baby's head,' she said, 'and there's the heart.'

Sheree couldn't make it out, but she had to believe her. After a while the nurse asked tactfully, 'Is there anybody else you'd like to show the pictures to?'

Sheree said, 'Yes, my husband, he's outside.'

The nurse apparently gave a sigh of relief, because she knew who I was but wasn't sure if I was the father. I suppose they have to be so careful. I must admit, I couldn't make the pictures out either, and we still couldn't believe this was really happening. I'll always remember the time when Dominic was about two and we were looking at him in his cot. Gazing down at him, Sheree said, 'Do you know, I'm still waiting for the knock on the door and for someone to say, "Right, we'll have him back now please"?'

When Doctor Barnett – who, incidentally, was a lovely man – confirmed that Sheree was pregnant, he said she'd have to come off her diet for the sake of the baby. That was the best news I'd ever heard. I'm sure that if she hadn't become pregnant she would have become anorexic, and who knows where that would have ended? God certainly works in mysterious ways. I know that's been said a lot, but in this case it was true and I'm sure that's why He wanted to give us a baby – our little miracle. And I think – no, I know – this miracle strengthened my belief in God. I also think my Mum had a word in His ear too!

We were working in Weymouth the year that Dominic was born (1988), and when it got near the time of the birth, Dr Gudgeon, who was Sheree's gynaecologist, knew I wanted to see the birth of the baby. Sheree was more or less ready to give birth, so he broke her waters, which is to supposed to speed up the delivery. Unfortunately, our plans didn't quite work out. By late afternoon it was obvious that Dominic wasn't going to come yet and the nurse informed me that it would most probably happen in the middle of the night. This suited my work schedule, because I would have been back by then.

That night I was on pins and towards the end of our last performance Eddie told the audience that Sheree was in labour and was about to give birth. At that very moment (it was 10.10 p.m. on 23 August), the Weymouth Ferry hooted its horn four times and Eddie said, 'That's it, the baby's been born!'

Well, would you believe it, when I got to the hospital they told me that Dominic had been born at 10.10 p.m! I was a bit upset that I'd missed the birth, but I probably would have fainted anyway. In the hospital all the nurses were smiling at me and saying 'Congratulations!', but I was preoccupied and just thanking the Lord for what He'd given us. Sheree went through a pretty rough labour, but she said she'd do it all again. Dominic was worth every bit of pain.

I can remember walking into the room the first time I saw Dominic and looking at his eyes. I had this overpowering feeling of love for him and I still couldn't believe that he was ours. We'd waited 14 long years and now we had this little bundle. He was nestled in Sheree's arms and you could tell that she didn't want to let him go. Her grip said, 'You dare take him from me!' But it was a lovely sight and we've got some beautiful photographs of that first night. It's amazing how something so small can mean so much to so many people. Sheree's Mum and Dad arrived and you could tell this was the one thing they wanted. I think they must have said a few prayers to God to give their daughter a little baby – and it worked. But most of all I think it made Sheree's life complete.

When Dominic was six months old we decided to have him christened at the church in Westhoughton where we'd married. He was also blessed at St Matthias in Torquay, and it was shortly after that event that I thought about being confirmed. Up till then I had always remained in my seat during communion. Sheree, Mum and Dominic would go up to the altar, but I just had to sit there. I'd been a Christian all my life, but I wondered to myself if I could still be confirmed at 50 years of age. To answer my question I went to see Peter, and he told me that of course it was possible. So a few weeks later I was confirmed, along with six other members. It was a lovely day and after the service we had a party. All the time I felt so good inside knowing that I was now a member of God's family – but there was still a lot of work ahead of me!

One of the things Peter taught me was that a Christian shouldn't be cocooned in his own little world. But in fact this is quite easy to do when you go to the same church every week and support the same charitable events and so on. Although it's a wonderful way of life, we should never forget that Christians are still dying for their faith in other parts of the world. Peter introduced us to Christian workers who had first-hand experience of these atrocities. Their stories helped us to keep life in its proper perspective, and I saw the benefit of listening to other Christians. One of the advantages of show business is that you can move around the country and meet other Christians wherever you go. Many that I've met have different views from myself, but I think that's quite healthy and it certainly helps us all to be more tolerant towards each other.

8

Warning signs

In 1991 Eddie and I performed in our last TV series after 14 years with the BBC. It was sad in a way, because when it was over we missed Bill Wilson, our fantastic producer and director who'd worked so closely with us. When your paths go in different directions you always hope that you'll keep in touch with people, but you rarely do. I still think about him and his wife Kath and their family and friends – if any of you are reading this book, get in touch! And when the series finishes you don't often see the working crew again – we tend only to meet now if Eddie and I are doing a guest spot on the *Generation Game* or one of the other quiz shows.

By the time we'd reached the last show in the series we'd virtually exhausted the format. It was time to move on. If anyone comes up with a new format, though, we'd love to do another series! Things were getting much harder in the last few programmes. You simply can't write everything yourself, and we were getting scripts that we'd previously refused, or we were doing things simply to fill air time. Having said that, though, 14 years on TV with your own series isn't that bad; I don't think many double acts have lasted that long!

I'm not sorry the '90s are nearly over now. I can't honestly say that so far they've been the best years of my life. There have been some really low points. One May afternoon in 1992 we'd invited some friends round and Dominic was playing outside as usual, and he seemed to be in a happy mood. But on the following day, a Sunday, we could tell there was something wrong. He was very quiet and lifeless and he wouldn't eat or drink.

We were really worried, so Sheree phoned the doctor and he came round. After examining Dominic he gave Sheree a prescription. He told us that it was a virus and that we should let him know if he wasn't better by Wednesday. By Wednesday Dominic's condition hadn't improved so we went back to the doctor, who said he should be taken to the hospital straight away. At the hospital Dominic was given an X-ray. Understandably, we were worried sick by now, because at just three years old he was the centre of our life (he still is).

The doctors admitted him for treatment immediately because the X-rays showed two big patches on his lungs. He had pneumonia. Sheree and I couldn't believe this. You always associate pneumonia with not being looked after, and living in damp conditions. The news really upset us both.

When the doctor came round to put an intravenous drip into his hand she missed the vein, so she had to try again. She tried five times, but by then Dominic was in a terrible state. As you can imagine, any child who has a needle stuck into them five times in a row would feel like a pin cushion, especially if nothing was happening as it should. Dominic was screaming with pain and I couldn't stand it. I know I'm a bit of a coward, but I had to leave the hospital. I'd rather they stuck the needles in me than Dominic. I walked out and left poor Sheree on her own. Eventually, the doctors said they had to get a needle in quickly because he was hyper-ventilating. Another doctor fortunately managed to insert one into his foot. Not surprisingly, this memory has left Dominic with a fear of needles. He can't even see one on television without panicking.

Whenever we went to see Dominic in hospital after that (he was in there for quite a few days) the doctors kept telling us that they couldn't go near him in their white coats. Apparently, they had to take them off and pretend they were normal people. If he saw a white coat he just freaked out. Seeing Dominic suffer was worse than my heart attack, but luckily, after a week he was back to his normal self.

Shortly after this drama Dominic had to start school. Sheree wasn't looking forward to this at all as she loves having him at home. I think she's the only mother who looks forward to the school holidays! I can still remember his first day and seeing him in his school uniform. Sheree had taken weeks to get it and because he's so small she had to alter everything. But you can only alter things so much. His hat must have been the smallest ever made, and his trousers still met his socks, even though they were taken up. They were far too big, but we couldn't make them any smaller.

Our neighbours, David and Wendy, came across to wave Dominic off for his first morning. Looking bleary eyed, they'd obviously got up early for the special event. On that momentous occasion we took photographs of Dominic before he left and it was so moving to see this little figure dressed up in his new uniform, and his mother so full of apprehension! I'll always remember that day because Sheree came back from the school and cried her eyes out. She just didn't want to be without him; in fact she still feels the same today.

Dominic's pneumonia attack was just the first of a series of 1990s low points. The tax man gave us a hard time, too, and then, in February 1993, Eddie and I had an exhausting weekend that I paid the price for. On the Thursday we flew out to Belfast to appear in a chat show. During the trip we met a great guitarist called Gordon Giltrap, who played in the evening but didn't finish until the early hours of the morning. Eddie and I had to get up early to catch a plane back to Manchester, then drive down to Northampton for a show. After that lot, I still had to drive back to Torquay.

When we were performing the act that Saturday night, I found I had difficulty remembering my role. There were big chunks of my performance that I couldn't remember at all. I know Eddie would say that wasn't unusual, but in all seriousness, it was. When we came off the stage he was blazing.

Well, you couldn't blame him, but I don't think his attitude helped me.

On my way home to Torquay I really didn't feel too good. The next day I woke up with a little pain in my chest. I brushed it aside, thinking it was probably indigestion. At lunch time I set the table and opened a bottle of wine, and still the pain was getting worse. But I said to myself, 'It's indigestion. I'll be all right after lunch.' After our meal I played with Dominic in the garden but I still didn't feel well. Sheree agreed that I looked out of sorts so she phoned the doctor and he came immediately. By this time the pain had spread down my arm.

Then the ambulance arrived and I thought I was a goner. I seriously thought I was on my way out. Strangely enough, I wasn't concerned about myself – it was Sheree who had me worried. Would she be able to cope and were our finances in order? Then my thoughts turned to Dominic and the possibility of him growing up without a daddy, and how I would not see him doing his growing up. This train of thought was making me feel depressed and I decided to stop thinking so negatively, and anyway I didn't want to die.

As the medical team carried me into the ambulance they put something under my tongue and an oxygen mask over my face. When I got to the hospital they gave me an injection of something that I later discovered is also used as rat poisoning! The injection was designed to deal with blood clots and it obviously worked because I'm still here. God obviously didn't want me to go just yet!

I spent four days in intensive care. On the first night the pain had subsided, but I still couldn't sleep. It was quite dark, with just a little light in the corner of the room, and then, out of nowhere, we had an emergency. Suddenly there were people everywhere and I realized that the man in the next bed had suffered a heart attack. The poor man was having a bad time and the staff were trying to resuscitate him. They were using electric shock treatment on his heart and I could hear the nurses trying to revive him. All the while I was thinking to myself, 'I don't want to hear this. Why can't I just lie here quietly?' and then I'd think, 'I hope he's still alive.' I found myself saying a prayer for him and hoping he'd pull through.

The next morning I looked across to his bed and he wasn't there. I felt very upset but I didn't ask about him because I didn't think it was the right thing to do. However, a month later, after I'd left hospital, I was going round a supermarket with Sheree and a lady came up to me and said, 'Hello, Syd, are you feeling better now?'

'Yes, fine thanks,' I replied.

'You might not remember me,' said this lady, 'but my husband was in the next bed to you in hospital,' and I thought, 'Oh dear.' But then I realized she was standing beside a man in a wheelchair and she said, 'Well, here he is!' I can tell you I was dead chuffed that he'd pulled through and was doing well. To be honest, at the time I never expected to see him again and now it seemed that my prayers had helped him.

When you're in intensive care it makes you realize why people feel it's important to fight for the NHS (okay, so I'm getting a bit political now...), because there's nowhere in the world you're so well looked after. I just can't praise Torbay Hospital (or any other hospital) enough because no matter what we say about this country and the way some things are managed, you suddenly become very grateful when you're as sick as I was.

In show business you simply can't afford to be ill because agents get very nervous. They say it's hard to 'sell you' if people think you're on your last legs. Inevitably, I had to recover as quickly as possible, even though the doctor had told me to have 10 weeks off. No one has 10 weeks off in this business! You're always back before you should be.

Strangely enough, death and illness are treated very lightly in show business. Any normal person would think we were cracking sick jokes, but in show business it doesn't seem to matter. When someone in the business dies, you'll always find a joke around. Our bad taste is always covered up by a remark like, 'Oh well, if he was around he'd laugh at that joke.' I used to think, especially when I was lying in hospital after my heart attack, 'I wonder what gags they'll be telling about me when I go?' Perhaps it would be, 'Have you heard that Syd Little has died, and Eddie didn't notice until he was halfway through the act?' I think I must have been in a bad way if these kinds of thoughts were passing through my mind!

When you suffer something like a heart attack you can be full of self-pity. Well, I was! There'd be times when I was thinking how close I was to dying and on those occasions I never considered the anxiety that Sheree and the family were going through. In fact, Sheree told me later that she'd broken down and cried, which is only natural. Dominic was trying hard to be brave. I remember him coming to see me a few times and he just stood there very quietly. Obviously his Mum had told him that I was very poorly and he should not make a noise. You realize when you look back how brave people have to be, and in the end it's the people you leave behind who suffer most. I'm getting morbid now! Anyway, I'd just like to add a word for Torbay Hospital: Thanks for everything, I can never repay you all.

That year (1993) our summer season was in Blackpool once again. I was feeling pretty much recovered by then, and we were on the bill with a guy called Joe Longthorne. Joe is one of those entertainers who has his own following. Wherever he goes the same people always turn up. Joe is well known, but he's not as famous as people like Shirley Bassey or Tom Jones. Mind you, I think he should be because he has such loyal fans. He's a bit like the Irish singer Daniel O'Donnell. Daniel may not be an international star, but he attracts capacity audiences. Well, Joe's just the same. Going to one of his shows is an experience because the first five rows are full of 'his' people, and not for just one performance. They'll probably have bought seats for the entire run. You can understand, then, why Eddie and I knew all their names. Joe's popularity also meant that after each performance the stage would be full of flowers, cuddly toys, and so on. Eddie and I got to know the fans so well that we received a few donations of our own!

In the show we did a routine of 'Singing in the Rain' at the end of the first half and, as the song suggests, we literally sang in a downpour! We did this twice a night, six nights a week for 16 weeks. One night in September we'd come to the end of the routine and the curtain came down and then went up again as usual – but instead of coming down for the second time it stayed up, and all the lights went on in the auditorium.

The audience were going wild and I thought, 'We should do this every night!' While I was trying to get the water off my glasses I looked down past Eddie – and all I could see were these green wellies. When I looked up I saw this big red book, and it was being held by none other than Michael Aspel. He turned to us both and said those famous words: 'Syd Little and Eddie Large, This Is Your Life!'

We later discovered that Sheree, Patsy, Dominic and Ryan knew all about this surprise as early as April. I'm sure it was very difficult trying to keep it a secret. After our performance we were driven from Blackpool to the Granada Studios at Manchester and the show was recorded at 1.15 a.m. When we arrived at the dressing room there was a bottle of red wine for me, a bottle of champagne for Eddie and our favourite chicken sandwiches. A fresh set of clothing was hanging up for each of us – no doubt organized by our wives.

Eddie and I were already on a high before we started the show, and when we stepped onto the stage everybody cheered. I have to tell you that we felt just great.

The strange thing about show business is that you might not see someone for years, then suddenly they turn up again. The last time we saw Michael was back in 1972, and here he was more than 20 years later, about to read our life story.

Although we didn't get much opportunity to chat because he had to dash off after the show, it was nice to see him again and he kindly left a message of congratulations.

After the show we had a party with all our mates, which went on till about 6.30 a.m., and I have to admit that I was the last to leave. The thing that got me was that even all our workmates from our teenage years were there. We had a great time swapping memories and singing together. Norman Collier, a fantastic comedian, is in his element at a party and you could hear people roaring with laughter around him. Everyone wanted to chat to Kevin Keegan about football and you can imagine that Eddie was one of that group (talking about Manchester City, of course).

It was a truly unforgettable night. When you're the subject of a show like that you start to realize how many people actually like you, or admire what you do. As well as those I've already mentioned, we had people there like Frank Carson, who's been a mate for years and still is, Frank Bruno and Bernard Manning, who recorded his bit saying he was sorry he couldn't be with us but all *good* comics were working! Singing star Gene Pitney sent a message of goodwill, as did many more. It was wonderful to think that so many people had gone out of their way to pay a tribute to us and each contribution helped to make it a very special evening.

This is Your Life was a high point in a difficult year. Looking back at my heart attack and Dominic's pneumonia, it was as if I was being prepared for something worse to come – but I'll tell you about that in the next chapter. I remember one of the congregation from St Matthias coming round and telling us that the entire church had prayed for Dominic that Sunday. I was really moved to think that people I didn't know intimately were praying for my son. Their concern gave me strength and it helped to build my faith, because I really believe in the power of prayer.

It was during these difficult times that I felt I wanted to know God more, and to allow Him access into my everyday life.

That kind neighbour from St Matthias was one of two special people who came into my life in the early '90s. The other was a Christian called Chris Gidney, who works in a pastoral role with people in show business. He came to my dressing room one evening because he'd heard that I was a Christian and obviously wanted to know more. I was impressed with Chris because he didn't come through the door with a Bible in one hand and a cross in the other – I don't think we mentioned Christianity in that first meeting at all. Instead we talked about everyday things like my family and Eddie's family.

After a few visits Chris told me he was involved with what's known as the Christians in Entertainment Organization. The work concentrates on providing show-biz people with spiritual support such as Bible classes. Chris used to pop round during the summer seasons and pantomimes and meet artists who wanted to see him. He didn't push himself, but if you wanted a chat he was always there. It was like having a travelling church. I must say at this point that it's Chris and his organization who have helped me to grow in my Christian walk. I looked forward to our meetings and although he didn't 'Bible bash' or anything, he'd often give me Bible verses to read. I'd tell him my troubles and he was always able to find an appropriate verse. I have so much to thank him for.

In 1995 we decided to sell our home in Torquay and move back to Lancashire. It seemed that we were booked to appear in Blackpool for alternate years and most of our work was in the north anyway. The completion date for our home was in November, when we moved to Cleveley, just north of Blackpool. It's a great place to live, and we were lucky to find a good school for Dominic into the bargain. I was amazed to discover just how many show-business people live in the Blackpool area: Roy Walker, Keith Harris & Orville, the Roly Polys and, when he was alive, Les Dawson, and now Bobby Ball has moved to the area with his family. A lot of Sheree's family also live in Lancashire so we're closer to them now, and my sister still lives in Manchester.

So all our relations are now close at hand, but it seems that our work isn't. As soon as we moved, our work switched to the south all of a sudden. (I think it's called 'Sod's Law', if you'll pardon the expression...) Still, to a certain extent it doesn't matter where you live in this business. With all these new motorways it's easy to get from Land's End to John O'Groats.

I said that I felt my health scare was a preparation for something. Well, my son Paul had never been an easy child and I'd have to say that many of the meetings I had with him through the years brought a great deal of pain into my life.

But that wasn't the end of it. If I hadn't had such a loving family and my Christian faith, I don't know that I could have survived what was to come.

9

A time of tragedy

I haven't said much about my children Paul and Donna because, to be truthful, I saw very little of them, especially in their teenage years. People always blame difficult children on broken marriages, but in Paul's case he was a problem from the start. He was uncontrollable even before my marriage with Mavis ended. My Mum always said that we let Paul get away with murder, and looking back I think she was right.

She often reminded Sheree and me about the occasion when Mavis and I went round to her house with Paul and Donna and they both had packets of Smarties. Paul had finished his so he took Donna's and ate all of hers too. And we let him get away with it because we didn't take Donna's packet away from him.

When the two of them came to stay with Sheree and me during the summer you'd hardly have known Donna was there, except for the times when Paul teased her. We tried very hard to make the holidays enjoyable, but they always ended the same way. Every time Sheree and I were glad to give Paul back to Mavis.

I can remember one incident when Paul was giving us a bad time in the car. The four of us were driving back to Mavis after spending some time together. Paul was in the back seat, hitting Donna and generally having a go at her. He was constantly threatening what he was going to do to her. Sheree and I kept telling him to be quiet, but it was such hard work. When we finally arrived at their house, Paul got out, said, 'Bye,' and then went inside. He started screaming at his mother and swearing really badly. Mavis rushed out and said, 'You'd better do something with him. He's going berserk in there!' She was right: he was going bananas.

By now I'd reached the limit of my patience. I'd coped with his bad behaviour all the way home and now I couldn't take it any longer. I stormed into the house, ran up the stairs, grabbed Paul and found myself literally throttling him. I really was getting out of control – he'd caused something in me to snap. Fortunately, Mavis and Sheree arrived and pulled me off. After a while I calmed down and came back to my senses. It was extraordinary how Paul seemed to know exactly how to wind you up to breaking point.

When Paul was 14 years old we took him and Donna to Blackpool for two weeks. We stayed in a hotel and I gave them each £5 a day to spend. After 20 minutes Paul would always come back and say, 'Can I have another fiver?' and I'd refuse. He'd then start swearing and storm off. He also started to smoke in front of me. I'd tell him to stop, but he'd just respond with a load of abuse. All this was particularly embarrassing because guests in the hotel recognized me and knew Paul was my son. On the other hand, Donna – bless her – kept the £5. I think she went back with more money than she came with because she wanted to save it. She'd window-shop with Sheree for ages until she finally selected a little bit of bric-a-brac.

Not too long after this trip a tax inspector came to see me about my tax returns. He was querying some figures regarding 'that' hotel in Blackpool and told me that I couldn't really pay for the trip out of company money – I needed to cover it personally. He asked me about the hotel. Was it The Warwick? When I said it was, he commented, 'I've been there. You had a problem with your son, didn't you?'

Well, I was shocked. It hurt to hear a total stranger say that to me. Now even the tax man knew that my son was difficult, and he was only 14. Where was it all going to lead?

Paul certainly had a habit of spoiling everything, but there was one summer in Bournemouth that was different. Paul had taken up fishing so he decided to bring his tackle with him. I'd find places for him to fish and he'd spend the day on his own. If there was one point in time that I could recapture with him now, it would be during one of those trips. Sheree and I dropped him off by the river and watched as he set up the tackle. Once this was completed he sat down on his basket and just looked so lonely. I wish now that I could go back to that day. I wish I could sit down beside him on that basket and that we could chat together. That was about the only holiday when we didn't have a cross word. I think it must have been because we hardly saw him!

After that summer Paul's behaviour got worse. Mavis didn't want to worry Sheree and me about the things he did, and if the papers had found out it would have been plastered all over them. But events took a sharp decline when Paul returned from a trip to America. He'd stayed there for about four months and when he came back he brought a sawn-off shotgun that he'd smuggled through in the back of a ghetto-blaster. Naturally Mavis told him to get rid of it, so he decided to take it to a police station. I don't know why, but he chose to go to Nottingham. You can imagine their reaction when a young man walks in with a shotgun! It didn't go down very well.

Paul was arrested and asked what he was doing with the gun. He said he was going to rob a bank to pay off all his 'debts and the rest of the money would be for Russian dissidents. It was this bizarre statement that made me realize Paul was far from well. He was eventually committed to a mental institution in Leicester and diagnosed as schizophrenic.

Eddie and I were in panto at Nottingham during Paul's confinement, so I was able to get over to Leicester to see him. Every time I saw him his mental state appeared to be getting worse. I was worried because the people around him seemed so poorly and I didn't think Paul was that bad. Was this the right place for him to be?

The first time I went to the Leicester Mental Institute it was a frightening and unnerving experience. The institute is set in its own grounds and it's a really old building. It must have been built in the nineteenth century and it reminded me of a movie set, with big gargoyles over the front entrance, huge doors and massive windows. It certainly wasn't very welcoming! The main building was full of offices and so on, but no longer provided accommodation for the patients. They lived in Portakabins and a range of more modern buildings in the grounds. The whole set up was somehow quite scary. It was hard to believe that people actually lived there – no wonder they made little progress!

I remember seeing Paul outside, sitting on a bench chatting to this little old lady. He gave her a cigarette, and then he saw me. 'Oh there's my dad,' he said to this lady, 'I'll see you later.'

Then he came over to me. I asked him who the lady was and he said, 'Oh, that's so-and-so, and she's 92.' (I can't remember now what her name was.)

'Ah, that's a shame,' I said.

'Yes, she's got no relations, no one comes to see her and she's very lonely. She's been in here since she was a little girl of about six. She was put in here because she was unruly and she eventually snapped. The place itself probably made her that way.'

It worried me that Paul was defending these people, and it seemed to me that he was starting to become like them. I'm sure that type of environment can make people worse. I felt so sorry for Paul and couldn't help wondering why he was in such an awful place and why he couldn't just walk out.

Eventually he was moved to Prestwich Mental Institute near Manchester. I was into painting pottery and ceramics at that time, and I thought it might help Paul if I could get him interested in the hobby too. I went to the institute to visit him, hoping to talk to him in a positive way. I went through about four sets of security gates, signed my name and walked across a very depressing yard – it was another old Victorian building. I then pressed the button on another door for a security check and walked up some stairs. At the top I looked through a glass panel and saw Paul. It was then that I thought to myself, 'That's not my son.' I really felt that I was losing him, and that perhaps he was losing the battle over his sanity.

I knew he was on medication, which was bad enough, but every time I went to see him he was only interested in cigarettes and whether I could give him some money. He was after money all the time. Despite all this, I felt so sorry for him. What a state to be in. After my visit I'd walk over to my car and just sit down and cry. Even today, after all these years, it still hurts me to think about that time. After I'd cried, I'd always pray for him.

After a few months Paul was released, which with hindsight was the wrong decision. But then Paul could charm the birds out of the trees when he put his mind to it, and his method obviously worked with the institute too. I later learnt that he'd been on drugs from an early age. I'm still quite naïve about drugs and I honestly didn't realize he was taking them. I remember Donna telling us that she'd been taught how to roll a joint at school, and how to recognize the different drugs. She was only 13 years old at the time! Sheree and I were amazed, but I suppose that's what they do at school now to try to educate children and stop the drug problem.

It would take a separate book to tell you the full story about Paul because there were so many incidents in his life. When he left Prestwich he stayed with a couple who volunteered to look after him. But he soon alienated himself from them and they kicked him out. Shortly after this, my knowledge of his whereabouts becomes a bit vague, but I do know he was into drugs in a big way.

On one occasion he came to Wimbledon, where Eddie and I were appearing in pantomime. Paul walked in with a man I didn't recognize and started to tell me he was in trouble. He told me that he'd stolen some jeans from a shop and he thought that with his record he'd be put in prison, so before he was arrested he wanted a holiday. We were talking in front of this stranger, who I later discovered was from the press. Paul was asking me for money while I was trying to tell him that he couldn't run away: he had to face the music. I said that I'd help him in any way I could, but he just kept on about the money. In the end I agreed to give him some money the next day. We carried on chatting about how he could get back on the straight and narrow, but I knew I was talking to a brick wall.

The following day I met him at the stage door. I gave him about £400 and said, 'You've got to spend this on a holiday, nothing else!' Unbeknown to me, across the road in a car were two photographers from a certain newspaper that I don't want to name. They were taking pictures of me.

Next day the headlines read 'Syd Little, Pay-Off – Get Out Of My Life, He Says To His Son', or words to that effect. I was gutted. To think that my own son had set me up and allowed the press to pay him for the story. All the time I was trying to get him to do something legitimate, and here were the press helping to feed his habit with lies. Even Eddie, who'd been Paul's champion for quite a while and had a lot of sympathy for him, couldn't understand why he'd done this to me. I think he fell out with him as well then.

I found it very hard to forgive Paul after that incident. Then one night, towards the end of January 1995, Sheree and I were getting ready to go out. It was our friend Kath's birthday. I was in the bath when the telephone rang, and Sheree answered the call from my sister Linda. Sheree came to tell me that Linda had phoned to ask me to call Mavis, as she had something urgent to tell me. 'Oh no,' I said, 'it must be something to do with Paul. I'm sure he's in trouble again.'

I asked Sheree to give Mavis a ring. The next minute she came running up the stairs and into the bathroom again and said, 'I don't really know how to tell you this, Syd, but there really is only one way.'

Paul had been found dead in a hotel room in Bangkok. At first I thought that this was one of Paul's ruses to get money and he was probably just in trouble and thinking of ways to get help. Looking back I don't know what I was thinking. It was one of those situations that you can't get to grips with immediately – it was as if the facts just wouldn't sink in.

I got on the phone to Mavis and she gave me all the details. Paul had been found in a hotel room with some needles stuck in his leg. He'd died of a heroin overdose. The news just made me feel numb inside.

The authorities sent me letters asking if Paul was to be buried in Bangkok or flown back to Britain. I had a chat with Mavis and she definitely wanted him to be buried back home. So I put the wheels in motion and eventually, after about four or five weeks, his body came back. A post mortem had been carried out in Bangkok and then they'd prepared the body for the flight. When the body arrived I was asked if I wanted to see it, but I declined. I decided that I preferred to remember Paul as he'd been in his younger days rather than as a drugs' victim. Although I didn't want to see him, Mavis decided that she did. She wanted to make sure it was her son and that he really was dead, because when someone dies so far from home there's always the possibility of mistaken identity.

In the church on the day of Paul's funeral I found that I was quite composed. I found a seat beside Sheree and we talked away to relatives and friends. I suppose my emotions were really confused and in a way I didn't know exactly how I felt. How do you cope when your son's body has been flown back from abroad and you think how young he was and what a waste his short life had been? I remained quite detached and numb until his coffin arrived. Then I just broke down. It was as if all of a sudden the truth hit home and I knew my son was really dead. Today, several years later, the memory of Paul still hurts.

The burial took place in Sale cemetery, by the railway line and the canal. The plot is about 100 yards from the site where Paul used to fish as a boy. It's strange, because when my father used to come home from work on a summer's day, he'd say, 'Right, I'm off fishing,' and he'd fish more or less in that same spot.

There were a lot of people standing round the graveside that day, including several of Paul's friends, and during a time of prayer we looked up and saw a huge rainbow. On that bitterly cold day it seemed as if Paul was talking to us through that rainbow and telling us that he was okay now. It was a strange spectacle for that type of day, and I think you often try to read things into unusual signs. It certainly seemed meaningful to me.

It's always been a great comfort to me that Donna and Sheree have maintained their close relationship, which began when Donna was just three. I can still remember Sheree showing me her make-up when she found little fingermarks in the powder pack. They were obviously Donna's and she must have been experimenting. We have many, many happy memories with Donna, but sadly she suffered because of Paul. He dominated every conversation and because he was always in trouble we tended to pay less attention to his sister. When Paul was younger, we tried every possible means to sort him out. He was expelled from school and because we didn't want him to be sent to a special one, we paid for a private education. This lasted just two months because he was expelled again. With hindsight, perhaps we should have concentrated more on Donna and paid for her education instead – but it's easy to be wise after the event.

During their teenage years we didn't see that much of either Paul or Donna, as I've said. When we heard from Paul it was always in connection with some sort of trouble, but Donna just got on with her life.

At Paul's funeral I was introduced to Donna's boyfriend – a French Algerian. Instinctively I was very wary of this man, because he was a surly character and it seemed to pain him just to say 'hello'. Three months after the funeral I took a phone call from our agent, Peter Prichard, and he asked me about Donna and whether I'd heard anything about her.

'What do you mean?' I asked.

'Well, she's been mugged,' he replied.

I doubted that this information was accurate so I decided to phone Mavis, but there was no reply. I then tried my sister Linda, who said she hadn't heard anything about Donna. To be on the safe side I eventually thought I ought to phone the police. They informed me that Donna had in fact been involved in 'an accident'. Wanting to know more, I eventually managed to track Mavis down. To my horror, it turned out that Donna hadn't had an accident: she'd been attacked by her boyfriend and now she was lying critically wounded in Wythenshawe Hospital.

While I was on my way to the hospital one of the staff called on my mobile to warn me that the press were waiting. They'd obviously got wind of the attack and wanted my reaction. Being sensitive to the occasion, the staff knew I just wanted to see my daughter, so they arranged a small detour for me, bless them! We met at a hotel outside Manchester and I was escorted in a mini-van through a back entrance.

As I approached Donna's corridor the nurse said to me, 'Do you know, and are you ready for what you're about to see?'

'No,' I replied. How bad was it?

She warned me that Donna's appearance might distress me and that I would need to prepare myself for a shock. Well, I thought I was quite a strong person so I continued down the corridor, but when I saw Donna's bed in the corner I just broke down. The nurse very kindly guided me into a side room where I cried my eyes out. I'd caught a glimpse of Donna and I could see that she was in a terrible mess. She was covered in bandages – in fact you could hardly see her – especially round her neck, and she had very thick ones on her hands.

Eventually I managed to pull myself together and listened to the full story of what had happened. Apparently Donna's ex-boyfriend had asked to see her for one last time – he was an illegal immigrant and was due to be deported within a fortnight. There was no real reason for this meeting because she'd finished with him by then, but he said that he just wanted to see her one more time. She agreed to meet him in his flat. When she arrived he asked if she'd like a cup of tea and then he disappeared into the kitchen while she sat down to watch the television. The next thing she recalled was feeling a moist sensation around her neck and then falling to the floor bleeding.

As he ran out of the flat, leaving her to bleed to death, she cried out, 'If you love me you'll tell somebody!'

Luckily, he told the taxi station downstairs to get an ambulance. 'I've murdered Donna!' he shouted, and off he went.

The lady from the taxi firm ran upstairs and found Donna on the floor. Her quick thinking probably helped to save Donna's life, because she wrapped towels around her throat, and every other part of her body that was bleeding heavily. By the time the ambulance reached the hospital she'd lost 12 pints of blood and was critically ill. Her ex-boyfriend had cut her throat twice then stabbed her down the back. The surgeon told me that the blade had just missed her spine – it had gone within an inch and a half of her heart and had pierced her lungs. She was lucky to be alive.

In addition to the wounds to her vital organs, she'd nearly lost one finger. During the attack Donna had raised her hands to defend herself and he'd slashed her fingers. One was almost severed, and the remainder needed micro-surgery. While the surgeons were concentrating on saving her life, however, her hands remained heavily bandaged.

Two days after my first visit Donna had some of the bandages taken off, and although she was highly sedated and couldn't talk, she was awake. Sitting at her bedside, I could tell she was pleased to see me.

'Well Donna,' I said, 'I've only seen this sort of thing in the movies! I've never seen it in real life before.'

'Oh,' said the nurse, 'Donna doesn't want to be in the movies.'

But Donna's big eyes lit up and her expression seemed to be saying, 'Yes I do! Yes I do!' I knew then that she was going to pull through. I think she'd love to be in show business. The nurse was so surprised because she communicated very clearly with her eyes.

A few days after that incident the nurse told Sheree and me that Donna was able to speak, so I went to see her. I think I was the first visitor to hear her voice after the attack. And I was so surprised, because the first thing she said was, 'Dad, I loved him!'

Well, what can you say to that? She asked me why he'd done this awful thing to her and I couldn't give an answer. Apparently he'd jumped the country after the attack and escaped to Northern Ireland. He'd stolen Donna's car to get to the airport and then flown to Belfast. He'd also removed her cash card from her bag and, as he'd obviously known the pin number, he'd wiped out her savings. The police reckon he's now in France.

During the investigation the police found a receipt for a set of kitchen knives that had been bought the day before Donna's visit. Why did he do this? He must have intended to kill her, deliberately buying the knives. The only possible explanation is that he thought, 'If I can't have her no one else will.' Perhaps we'll never know – he still hasn't been caught.

Eventually Donna was well enough to move to Withington Hospital for the micro-surgery on her hands. The extent of the damage involved months of surgical work, and even today she's still recovering both mentally and physically. But there are definite signs of improvement. On the outside she's still a bubbly person and every time we see her she appears very happy, but on the inside I feel it will take some while for her to find real happiness again.

After Donna had been released from hospital she came to stay with us in Blackpool. She could get about by then, but she had difficulty breathing because her lungs had been pierced. Her hands were still bandaged and Sheree used to bathe them for her. I was comforted to see Donna at home with us all and I felt sure there was an extra-special bonding between us during that time. After a fortnight she returned to Mavis's house, where she's currently living. She has told us that she still suffers from nightmares and that she's definitely off men for at least a year!

I know I couldn't have wished for a better daughter and we all love her dearly. One aspect of my relationship with Donna that's really pleased me is her feeling for Dominic. It's wonderful because at first he didn't know he had a big sister, and for a while he was too young to understand. But now when people ask him if he has any brothers or sisters he says, 'Yes, I've got a sister,' and he's very proud of the fact. We're so pleased that Donna is in close contact with us these days.

Through all these traumas Sheree was a pillar of strength to me. Without her I wouldn't have survived. Just one incident like this would have been enough in a lifetime, but to have suffered two in the space of two months was almost impossible to bear. Knowing she was there to support me stopped me from going under.

I often ask myself why it should have been that Chris Gidney from Christians in Entertainment came into my life just before these tragedies. It was as if I was being sent a special helper from God. Looking back, I can see that he was also there to help me through those traumatic months. Chris and his assistant Sally Goring both phoned me to say, 'Our prayers are with you and your family, Syd.'

It was great to have their concern for me, but I still thought, 'God, why have you sent all this trouble to me? Why do I have to cope with all this? Why my Paul and Donna?'

These aren't easy questions to come to terms with, but I always say, 'If you believe in God you must believe in the devil.' It was obvious to me that the devil was at work where Paul and Donna were concerned. But now I know that God has been at my side when I've been in trouble – and He was definitely protecting Donna. Right now I just want to go on believing that He'll always be there in the future.

10

Faith for the future

There's a poem I found some time back which always moves me. It's called 'Footprints', by a lady called Margaret Fishback Powers, and it must be one of the most popular Christian poems of all time. It says so much in so few words. Do you know it? She dreams that she's walking along a beach with God, and scenes from her life flash across the sky. In each scene there are two sets of footprints, one for her, one for God. But then she notices that at the hardest times in her life, when she was in real difficulties, there's only one set of footprints to be seen. Where was God in those times of trouble? I think the answer God gives in the poem is just great:

He whispered, 'My precious child,
I love you and will never leave you
never, ever, during your trials and testings.

When you saw only one set of footprints
it was then that I carried you.'

Looking back at my life there have been many times when I've seen just one pair of footprints instead of two. Life on the whole has been very good to me, but since I let God back into my life it does seem calmer – I can feel a strength there that I couldn't find before. And my faith has led me into all sorts of new experiences!

In 1997 Sheree opened a guesthouse in Blackpool (although she's now stopped running it) and it was surprising just how many committed Christians came to stay. We even had three nuns! You might think that nuns would be rather dull people and that you'd have to be careful what you say. Well, my experience proved exactly the opposite because we had a great time with Sister Bernadette. She arrived with her mother, and one evening she got hold of my guitar and started to sing a few songs. She didn't bother with the one everyone associates with singing nuns – 'Dominique' – but instead she chose a selection of Liverpool ditties – including 'Maggie May' and 'In My Liverpool Home' (which she taught me how to play). She was such a happy person and I really enjoyed her company.

Then we had Sister Margaret and Sister Frances. A few weeks after their visit, and about a week after Princess Diana's death at the end of August 1997, we received a letter from Sister Frances thanking us for returning her pyjamas and telling us about her work in a northern prison. Because she conducted Bible studies in the prison, she'd discovered how touched the inmates were by Diana's death. She said that many were genuinely upset and grieving for her, and that boxes placed outside the cells had been filled with money and poems. Apparently they also wrote to Diana's mother. On another occasion a man who'd been convicted of armed robbery complained to Sister Frances about someone who'd pinched a teddy bear from a floral tribute outside Buckingham Palace. It takes all sorts and, as they say, 'Not all the guilty people are locked up in prison.' Diana's death was understandably a tragic time for the nation, but as Sister Frances said, 'We've already seen so much good come out of such horrific circumstances. A testimony of people displaying God's goodness amongst us.'

As I've said before, it's great being an entertainer because when you perform in lots of venues around the country, you can go to so many different churches. I especially like those with a lively atmosphere and if you're thinking of going back to church, or going along for the first time, do have a good look round. Just because there's a church at the top of your road, it doesn't mean that you have to go to that one. It's best to find a church which suits you and has a style you're comfortable with. I've discovered that churches can vary from very traditional services to the 'happy-clappy' ones (at least that's what I called them when I was young). Given the choice, I have to say that I prefer the 'happy-clappy' type – the Bible says in Psalm 33 that we should 'Give thanks to the Lord with the lyre; sing praises to Him with the harp of ten strings. Sing to Him a new song; play skilfully with a joyful sound.' It's good to celebrate.

Faith for the future

I'm still in the early stages of my faith, but I'm surrounded by so many encouraging Christians that it's all getting easier. I've also been reading a little booklet called *Every Day With Jesus*. Inside the booklet there are small passages of Scripture to read every day, with short explanations to help you understand what you're reading. Each booklet runs for two months. There are others like it on the market, and I'd really recommend choosing one of them to follow. I've found it's very helpful to read a little of the Bible every day.

When I'm out and about it's funny how often people come up to me and say, 'Are you Syd Little?' When I say, 'Yes,' they'll add, 'You're one of those "born-again Christians" aren't you?'

Well, I've heard this statement a lot, and at first I felt like I was suffering from some rare disease! I have to say that I did feel awkward about admitting to my faith, but now my confidence has grown and I find it easy to reply, 'Yes, I am' (although, as I said earlier, I don't really like the term 'born-again' – I prefer to think of myself as 'rediscovered'). I've learnt that witnessing for your faith is no big deal, especially when you compare it with the lives of the early Christians. If *they* admitted to their faith they died for it!

Even after all the tragedies in my life, including Paul's death, Donna's attack and Dominic's pneumonia scare, I've chosen to become closer to God. This has been in preference to walking away from Him, which many people might have expected from me. What I really enjoy about my relationship with God is that His presence can be felt in all sorts of places.

In 1996 Eddie and I went to the Falkland Islands to entertain the troops. For you younger readers, the Falklands are near Argentina, and in 1982 there was a war between Argentina and Great Britain, officially termed a 'conflict'. It was a serious situation and many people were killed. Mind you, if you ever visit the islands, you'll probably wonder what all the fuss was about! The phrase 'God-forsaken' sums up the place perfectly. There are no trees and it's so bleak. You actually feel sorry for the men who are stationed there for three months at a time. Between 20 and 30 of them are out on the mountain-tops working on radar control. Anyway, Eddie and myself, a singer and four dancing girls (especially for the lads) were sent to entertain them.

It was a great little troupe. The weather was so dreadful that we were stuck on this mountain for two days. The conditions were so appalling that the helicopter couldn't pick us up. But the troops did everything they could to look after us, and in the end we had a really good time.

Despite the weather and the barren land, I really felt the presence of God in the Falklands. I remember going into this little chapel on Mount Pleasant and finding it empty. Surrounded by just the bare essentials required for a church service, I sat and talked to God. I asked His advice about certain things and I felt He was very close to me. It was a strange yet comforting experience.

One of the funniest things I remember about the Falklands is a trip I took on a Hercules plane over a penguin sanctuary. As the plane descended in order for us to have a better look at the birds, the penguins followed us with their eyes and then promptly lost their balance. Well, if you can imagine thousands of penguins all falling over at the same time … it was a funny sight! Still, I'm glad I was up in the plane and not down on the ground because the smell was terrible. Let me tell you, penguins really do stink!

On the way back from the Falklands we stopped at Ascension Island because we'd been booked in for a couple of shows. While I can't remember the exact name of our venue, it was next to a chapel. It was a beautiful summer evening – the climate there is exactly the opposite of the Falklands because it's in the middle of the Atlantic – and I was feeling a bit down as I was missing Sheree and Dominic. Seeing the chapel, I walked over and tried the door. It was open so I walked in. This chapel had a welcoming red carpet and it was warm inside.

As I closed the door behind me, I felt again that God was in this place. I started to study the plaques on the wall dedicated to the young British sailors who'd been killed or had died from a disease – they all seemed so young. As I sat down, Paul came into my mind. And on that summer evening far from home, I felt that he was beside me. Somehow his presence there helped me, because I still felt a bit guilty about him. I do believe that he's in a better place now.

It's easy to get into an argument about God, your faith, Christianity and religion. Other Christians have advised me that you don't have to explain why you believe in God because God will defend himself – and that's good enough for me.

I'm reminded of a story about W.C. Fields, who was famous for saying things like 'I never drink water, fish make love in it', and 'Never work with children and animals'. He had a reputation for being irreligious. When he was on his death-bed, his manager went round to see him. Mr Fields was reading the Bible when his manager arrived.

The man couldn't believe what he was seeing, so he went over and said, 'Well, W. C., I'm amazed to see you reading the Bible.'

W. C. Fields looked at him and said, 'I'm looking for a loophole!'

I know a lot of cynics will say that I've jumped on a religious bandwagon, because a lot of entertainers have 'come out' and openly confessed their Christian faith – people like Cannon and Ball, Cliff Richard, and many others. But whatever way those artists came to the Lord, my own belief grew through the events that happened in my life. I'd also have to add that my faith grew strong because I was helped by people like Chris Gidney. I really hope that more people in my profession will openly confess their faith, because I'm sure there are lots who haven't done so yet. Believe me, it won't do you any harm. Take the people I've already mentioned: they're doing okay, aren't they? But regardless of your profession, if you feel you want to let Jesus into your life and then tell everyone what you've done, go ahead: do it!

Most of my immediate family are Christians and we try to attend church as much as we can. At the moment we go on a regular basis. My father-in-law says that you don't have to go to church to prove you're a Christian and to a degree that's true, but you miss out on fellowship if you don't, and the encouragement of other believers helps to strengthen you.

When I look back at my career with Eddie spanning 35 years, it's amazing to think how many Christians I've met. One of them was Roy Castle. We met Roy at a birthday party for Eddie down in Torquay and the two of them were standing in a corner having enjoyed a few drinks. Roy was saying to Eddie, 'Oh, but you're great,' and Eddie said to Roy, 'But you can play a trumpet, in fact any instrument you want,' and Roy replied, 'But you're great because you do all these fantastic impressions,' and so it went on. I can still remember them just praising each other. Later on when I talked to Roy, I sensed he had this inner peace – the same inner peace that I'd recognized when I met Cliff Richard.

In Blackpool in 1996 Chris Gidney, Jimmy Cricket, myself and a few others were trying to hold a Bible study in Bobby Ball's dressing room. Lapsing for a moment or two from our reading, we started to reminisce about club life. Then, all of a sudden and for no obvious reason, I felt I wanted somebody to pray for me. Bobby started to pray and asked God to forgive my sins and that just broke me up. From that moment I started to cry and, as they say, 'let it all hang out'. Afterwards I felt so much better, and that experience left its mark because I *still* feel better, even today. The outcome of that special experience made me want to be an even better Christian and to put myself in a position to help others.

During 1997 Chris Gidney asked me if I'd like to do a 'gospel tour', travelling around various Christian centres and churches in Britian. The idea was that Chris would feed me a few questions, so that I had the opportunity to share my testimony, and then I'd sing a few songs. To be honest, I wasn't sure that I was ready for the spotlight to be put on me, especially without Eddie, but Chris was confident that the time was right.

My first three bookings were for Eaglescliff, near Stockton-on-Tees, Glasgow and Wigan. Chris accompanied me on the tour, along with a smashing group called the Juliet Dawn Foundation – consisting of Dave and Juliet, who are married, and Patrick the drummer. Patrick is also the percussionist and he's very talented, as they all are. I particularly enjoyed Patrick's company because he's got a good sense of humour, so we were able to have some fun.

This tour was such a new experience for me because I'd never worked alone; I'd always had Eddie. Believe it or not, the thought of being on stage on my own was quite frightening. Having said that, though, I did have the back-up of Juliet, Dave and Patrick. On that first night at Eaglescliff I remember waiting in the wings while the group did their little piece, then Chris went on and did a few gags which went very well (I was upset about that!). And then it was my turn. I couldn't believe it: my knees were actually knocking! Up to that point in my career, even during all the television recordings and the big performances, I'd never felt so nervous. For the first time in my life I discovered that your knees really can knock when you're scared!

When Chris introduced me, though, I forgot about my knees and walked on to a great response. I sang a Buddy

Holly medley – 'That'll Be The Day', 'Peggy Sue', 'Raining In My Heart', 'True Love Ways', etc. Before the performance I'd told Chris I had a teddy-boy outfit with a velvet-collared jacket and some red shoes. He encouraged me to wear them because they were just right for the numbers I'd chosen. Anyway, it all went well and I was pleased!

After the medley Chris and I sat down and chatted about my life, and I gave an account of some of the incidents in this book. Then I sang another song, and we went on to talk about Paul and Donna. We ended our chat by talking about what God meant to me. To close the evening we sang a rousing rendition of 'What A Friend We Have In Jesus' and 'Love Shines A Light' (the 1997 Eurovision Song Contest winner), and this went down a storm. The last song was so fitting because God really does shine a light in our lives.

Overall it was a fantastic night and I met some lovely people after the show. I sat down at a table with Juliet while Dave and Patrick moved the gear off the stage, and we signed autographs and chatted to people. I'd never done anything like this before, but people were coming up and telling me, 'Syd, you really touched us with what you talked about,' and I couldn't believe what they were saying. One lady came up to me with her husband and told me that she went to church every Sunday and he didn't. Now, because of what I'd said, he'd changed his outlook on Christianity. He wasn't the only one: many more people came up with exactly the same response. To complete a very rewarding evening, we celebrated later over a curry (one of my weaknesses – just ask Chris!).

The next night the venue was Glasgow. This was a different kettle of fish altogether. Situated in the dockland area called Galton, the pastor had mentioned that the site was quite rough. In fact, after the show, the pastor and his wife apologized for missing the performance. 'We were outside looking after your cars,' they explained. Apparently there'd been a couple of suspicious people hanging around, so that gives you some idea of the sort of area it was. Having said that, the congregation was fantastic and I've never experienced anything quite like that night in terms of the response from an audience.

Eaglescliff, the night before, had been a very modern building and it looked as if a lot of money had been spent on it. The venue in Galton was an old town hall in a very dilapidated state. The organizers had done well to get it freshly painted, but it was still very old. When the concert started the congregation were immediately up on their feet, singing and really enjoying themselves, and after the show I went down to meet some of them.

I was really touched by one lady who came up and said that she could identify with Donna's experience because her boyfriend had beaten her up and then threatened her with worse. When I was originally asked to talk to her I thought, 'What can I say?' I found it very hard because people were asking for my advice and I'd no experience of this sort of thing – except what had happened in my own life.

A young lad called Graham asked if I'd pray for him and I said, 'What can I say for you?' He told me that he was a drug addict and that he understood what I'd been through with Paul. I prayed, asking God not to let him end up like my son. I hope my words got through to him, and that he managed to conquer his addiction.

I couldn't get over the fact that these people were asking me to pray for them, and asking my advice. It was a very emotional night for me and when it was over I felt pleased that I'd coped and grateful that God had helped me.

The third night we went to Wigan and had the concert in a 'proper' church. It was great because I went out to watch Juliet, Dave and Patrick, and their set looked fantastic. They were up by the altar and they'd assembled their own lights which shone down to great effect. With the advantage of good acoustics, Chris and I went on and did our bit, which again was well received. During that tour we'd performed in three completely different venues and each was special in its own way.

So that was my first gospel tour. Later in the year, during November, I did a couple of nights in Bedworth and Derby and they were equally good. I really enjoyed being a part of these tours and I hope I can do some more in the future. The influence Chris had on me was fantastic. He encouraged me to pray before every show and God always answered, because He gave us the strength we needed. And more than that, I hope we helped some other people along the way. Since that time when Bobby Ball prayed for me it's been my ambition to reach out and help others, and hopefully these tours have enabled me to do just that.

One of the questions Chris asked me on the tour was, 'What are the three things that help you to be a good Christian?'

I said, 'Well, I believe in the power of prayer so I pray a lot and I read my Bible. But above all, I think it's important to get involved with other Christians.' We've all experienced different problems, but when we allow God into our lives He's able to deal with them, and sometimes this can involve ministry from other Christians.

I think the combination of being a celebrity and a Christian is quite hard. You might not think so, but if you work in an office or as a tradesperson, people probably accept you and your faith without much question. But if you're well known in show business some people are bound to start saying things like, 'Oh yes, is your career on the slide then?' or, 'Tell me, why does God let all the bad things happen in the world?' as if you know everything because you're a public figure. But let's face it, none of us has all the answers. But I'm encouraged because for every non-believer I meet there are still 20 or more believers!

Sometimes I regret not letting the Lord into my life earlier, because I'm sure He would have helped me to cope better. Now I know He was there all the time and just waiting for me to let Him in. I remember going to see the film *Forrest Gump* a while back, and one of the characters said to another that his mother had told him life is like a box of chocolates: you don't know what you're going to get until you open it. Well, you could say the same is true about letting God come into your life!